ON THE FUNNY
SIDE OF THE STREET

by
RON OWEN

Spring View Publications
SpringViewPublications@outlook.com

All cartoons are Ron's original work
any similarity with any other published
material is purely coincidental

Typeset by Candy Evans
Cover design concept by Catherine Sharman
Printed and bound by IngramSpark
ingramspark.com

978-1-7398659-1-7

With thanks to

Ron's nurse Hannah Blunsdon,
the team at BBC Midlands Today,
Cyril Hobbins, Candy Evans and all others
who made this publication possible

FOREWARD

Ron and I were born in 1938 and we have been best friends since our wartime childhoods. Our fathers were absent, serving in the Army for six years, leaving our hard-working mums on their own with us young children.

Left to our own devices, we were forced to amuse ourselves. We both took to childish art, but in different ways. I was the traditionalist but Ron dived straight in to cartooning, learning by copying from a variety of places, especially Disney comics.

His skills with pencil and pen developed rapidly over the years and combined with his ready wit and good humour he could produce a funny cartoon at the drop of a hat. And still does.

Always a welcome...

Always a smile...

Cyril Hobbins
December 2021

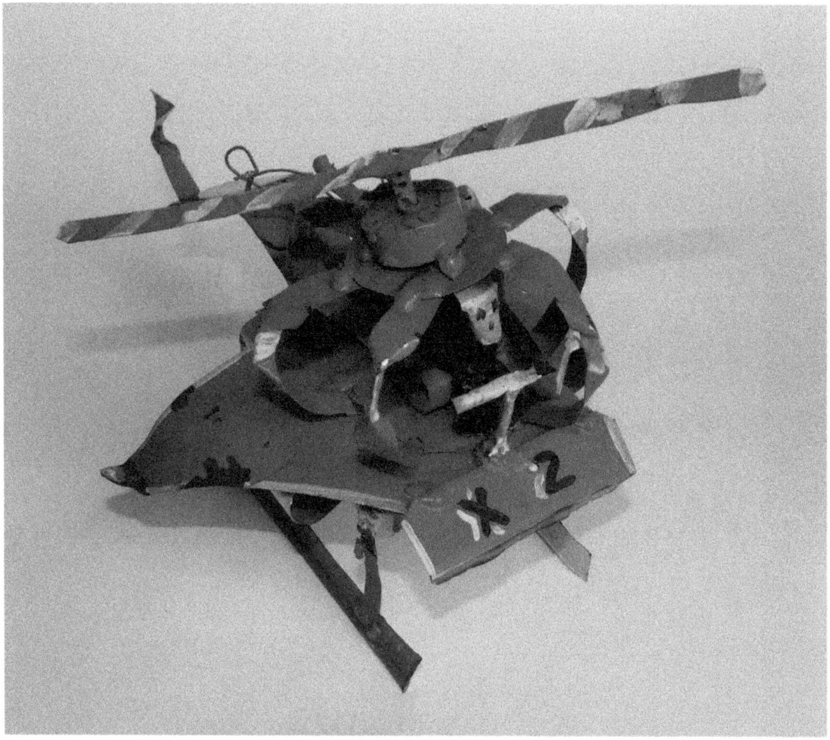
X 2

A solar-powered helicopter made by Ron
from an old Quality Street tin

INTRODUCTION

Ron Owen is a true folk artist with no formal art training.

He also produces unique, well crafted items from discarded tins – everything from model aircraft driven by wind or solar-power to whirligig windmills in insect or animal form.

In the past he was noted for designing and building incredible carnival floats and large Christmas tableaux for children's parties and businesses, in his home town of Kenilworth, Warwickshire. He is also a very talented sign writer.

Ron will produce a drawing at the drop of a hat and can often be found sketching on holiday, at home or abroad, creating something special in minutes.

He has gained many friends (not to mention the odd complimentary drink or meal) after sketching on a paper table cloth or napkin. Most such cartoons have been given away freely, not expecting any reward, except a happy smile and often a laugh.

We hope you enjoy this small selection of cartoons from his vast, ever-growing collection.

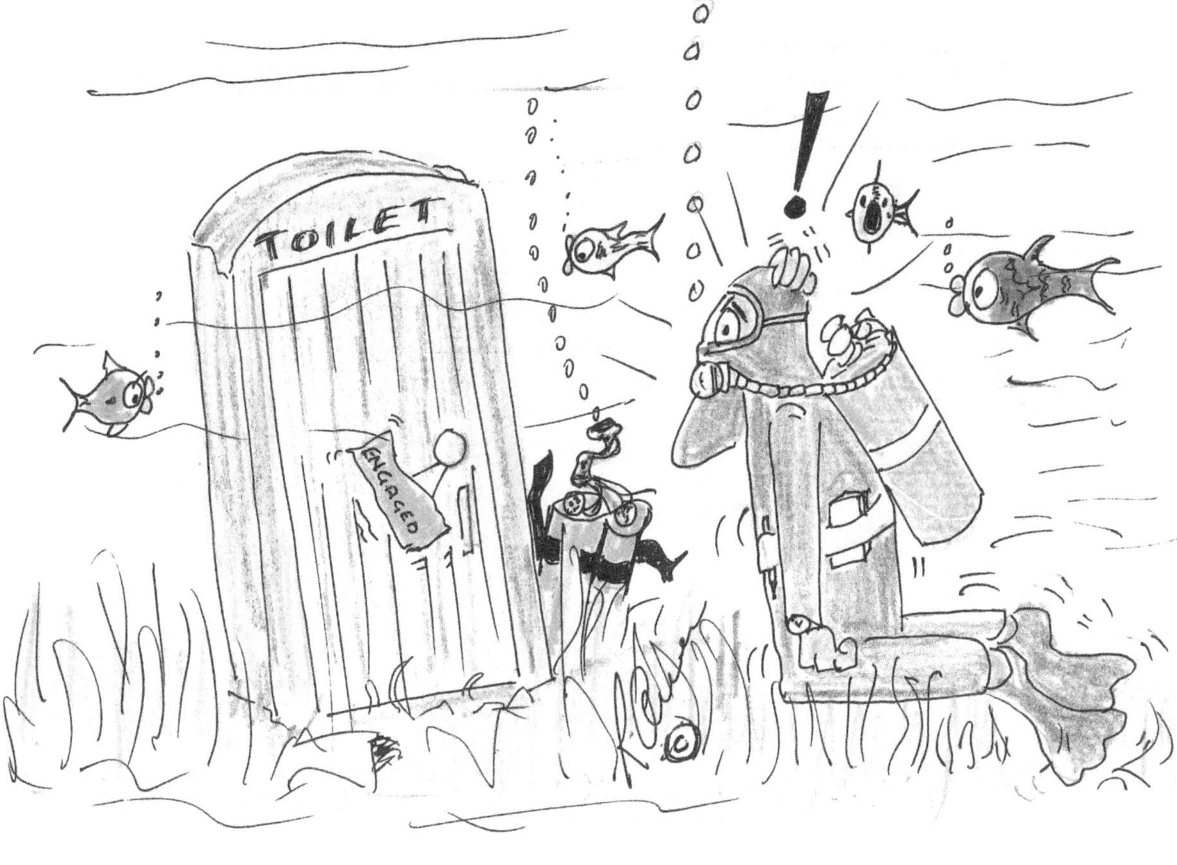
TOILET
ENGAGED
!

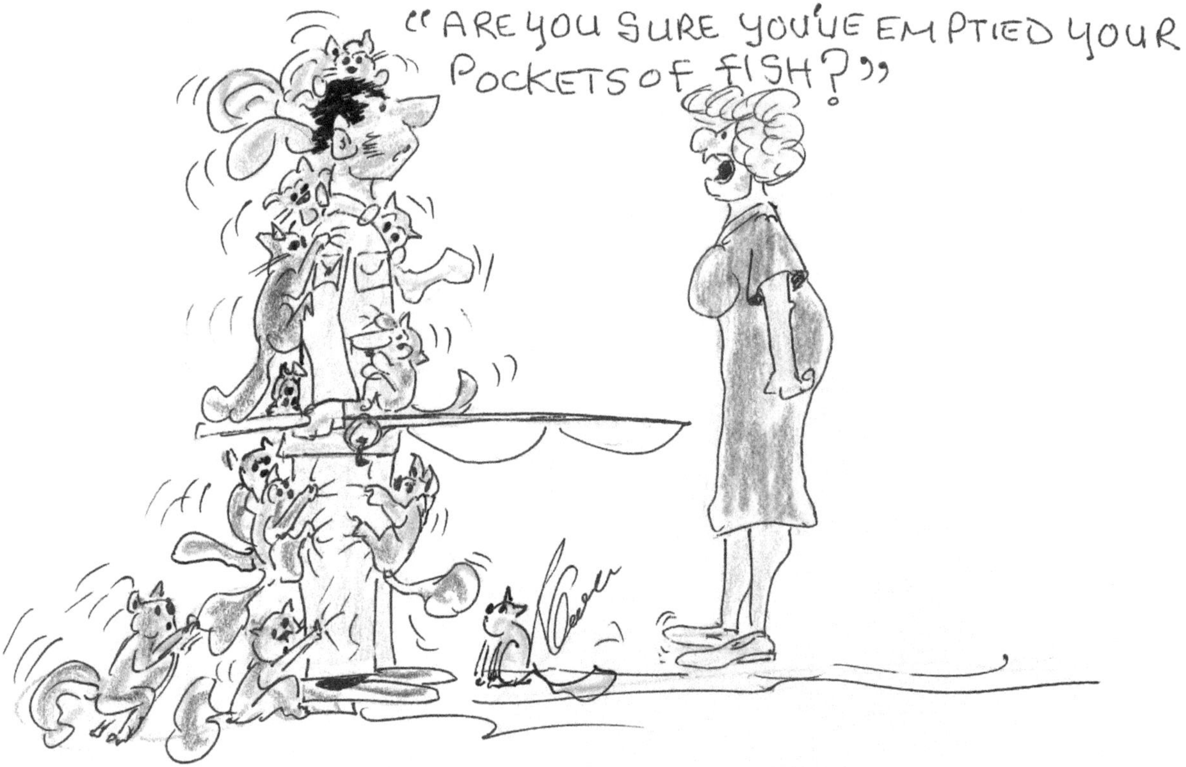
"ARE YOU SURE YOU'VE EMPTIED YOUR POCKETS OF FISH?"

"DIDN'T YOU CHECK THE BRAKES ON THE TRAILER TENT!"

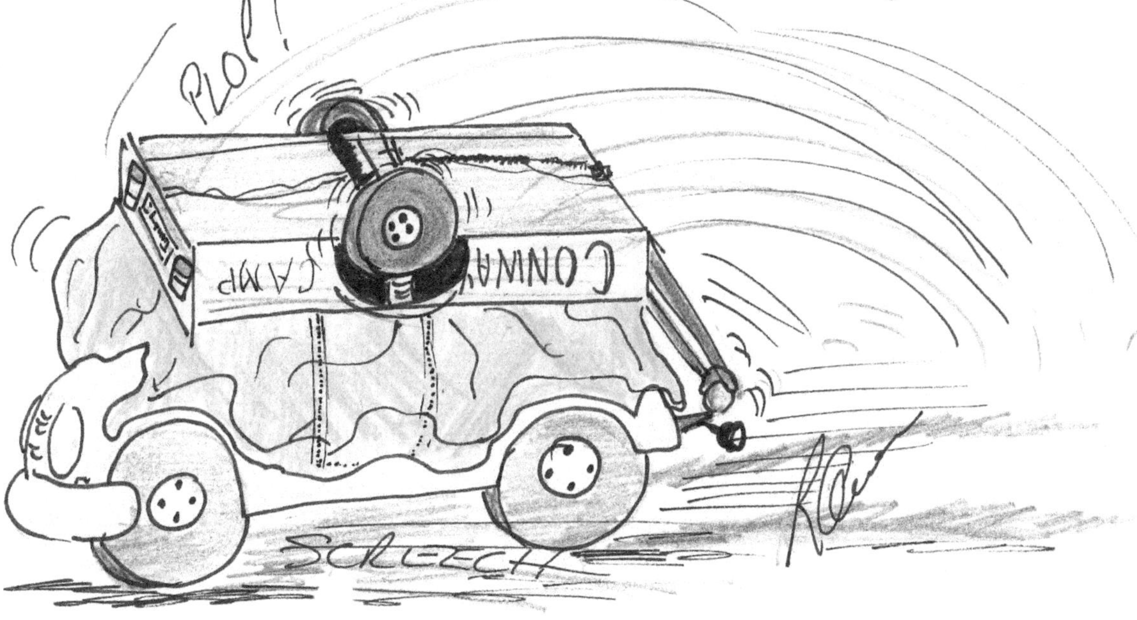
PLOP!
SCREECH

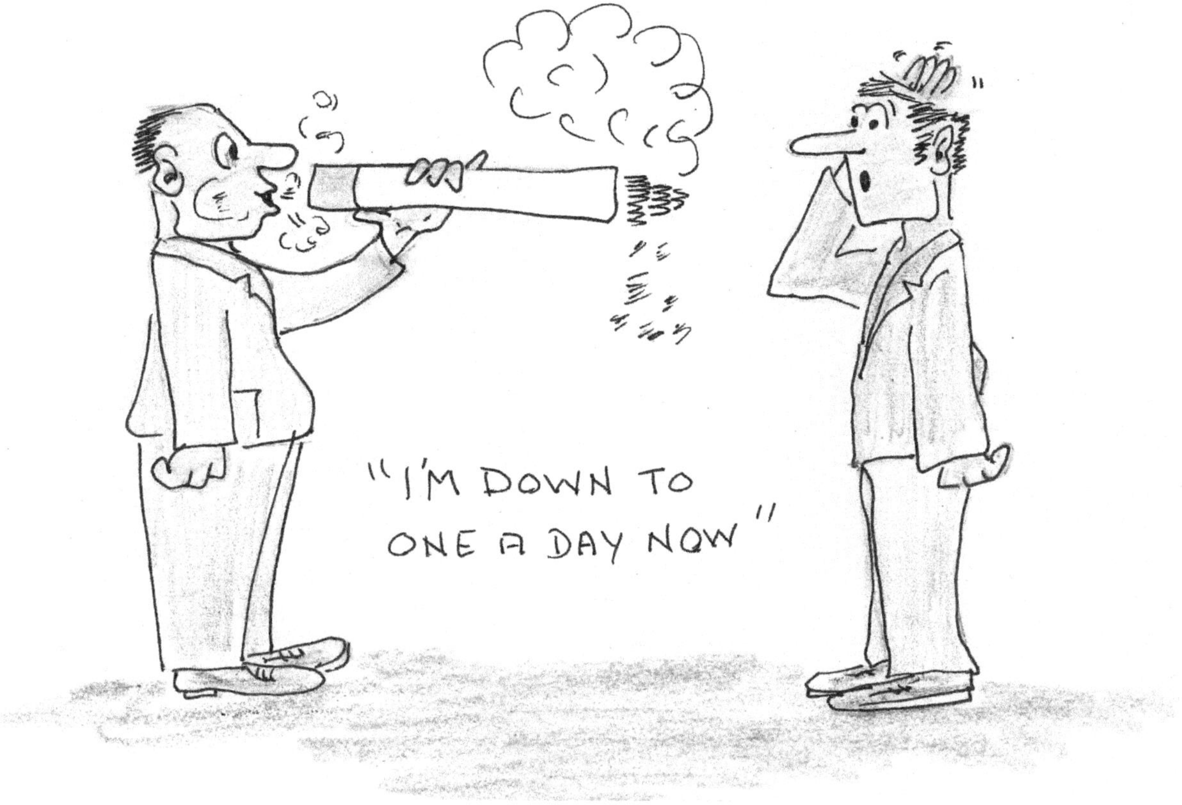
"I'M DOWN TO
ONE A DAY NOW"

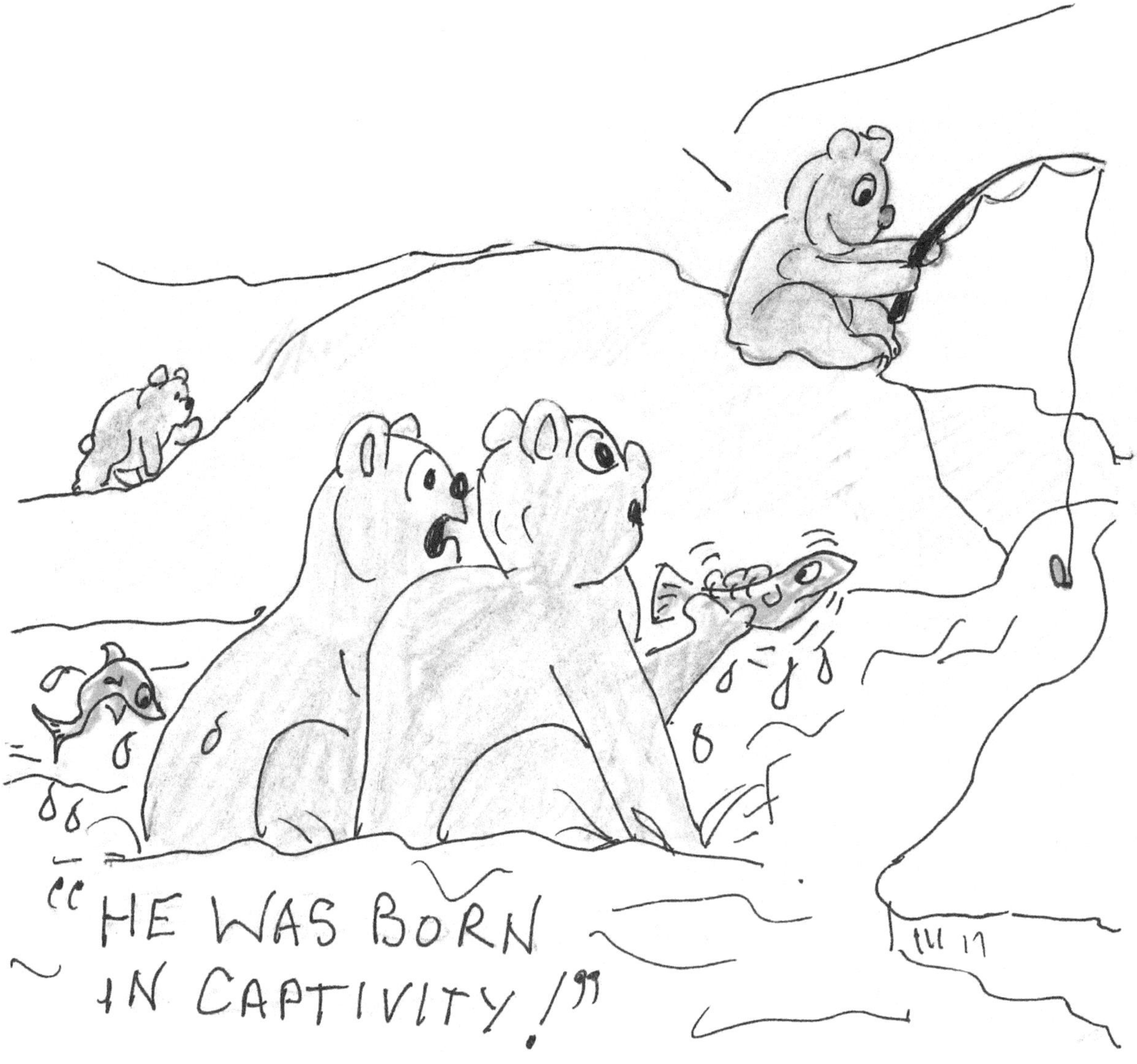
"HE WAS BORN IN CAPTIVITY!"

"THEY SAY IT TENDS TO FLOOD HERE!"

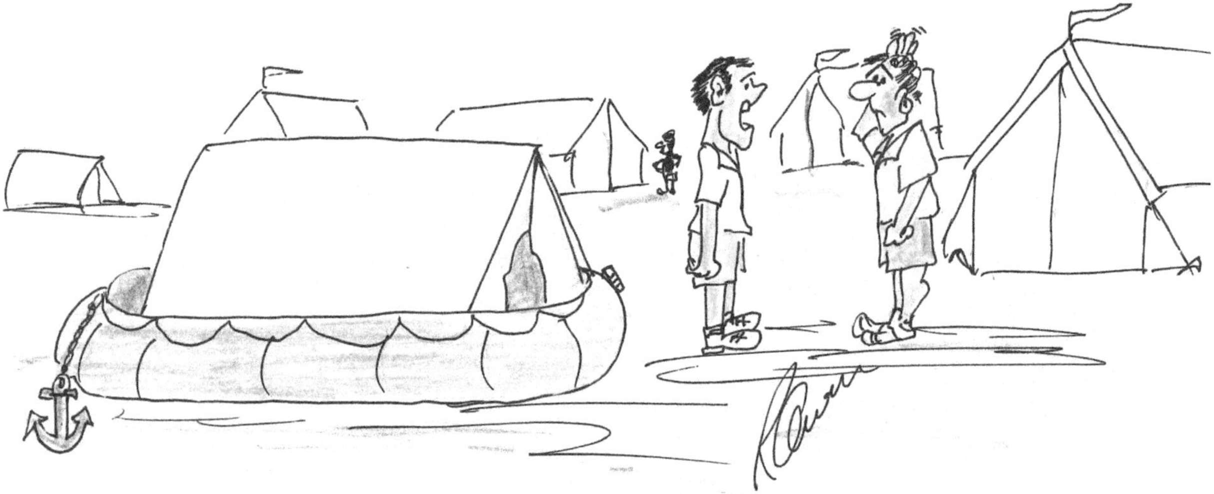

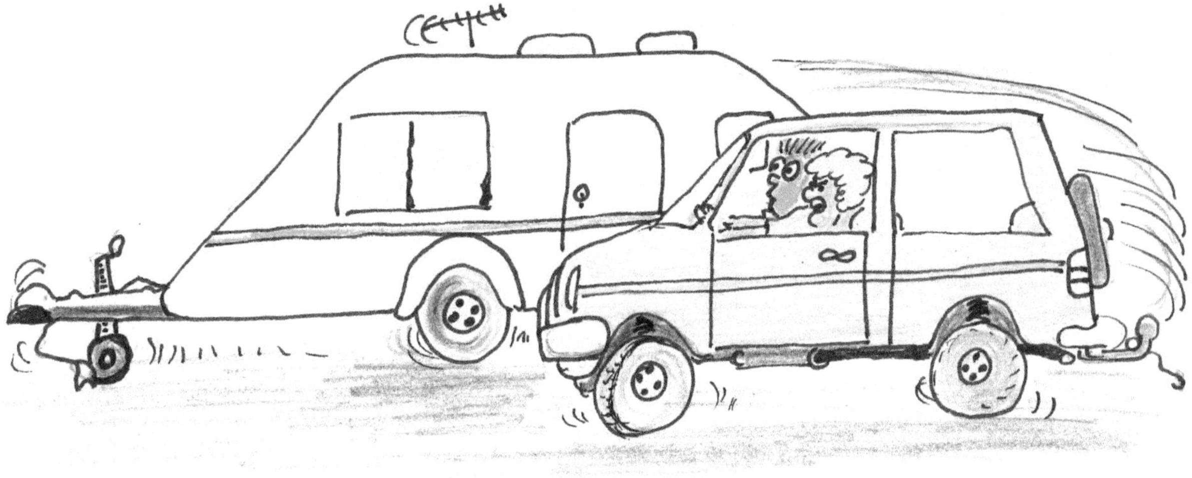

"THANK GOD HE'S GONE BY HE'S BEEN BEHIND US FOR HOURS!"

"I THINK WE SHOULD HAVE HAD A LONGER ROPE ON THE ANCHOR SID!"

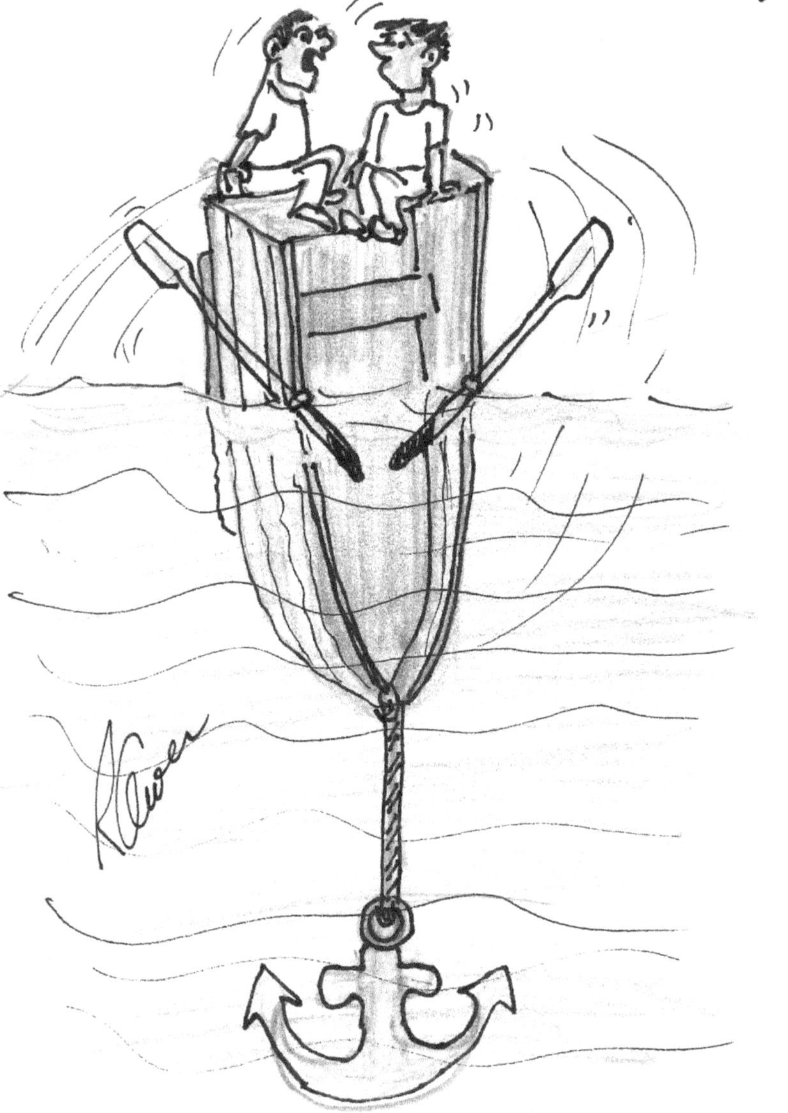

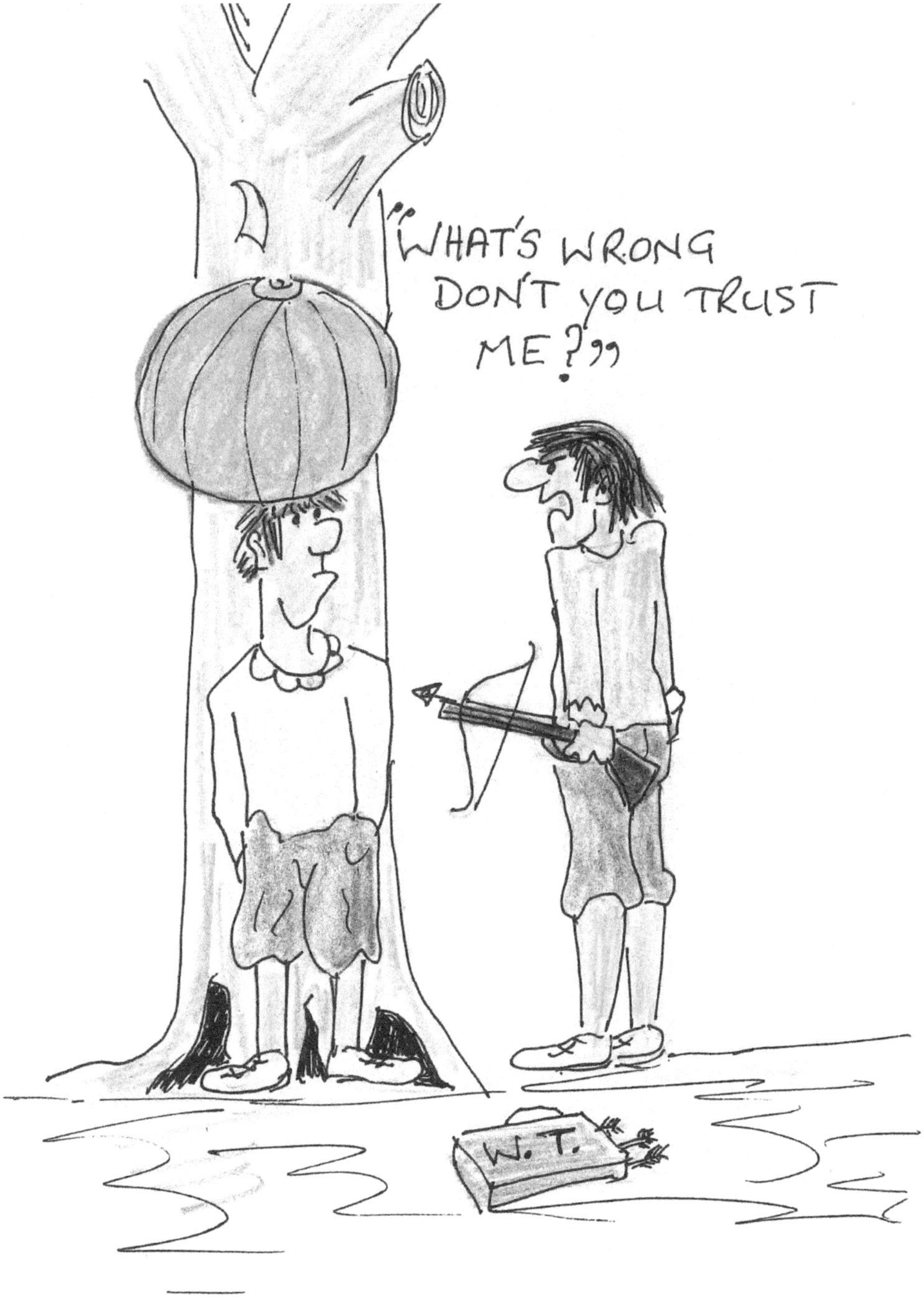
"WHAT'S WRONG DON'T YOU TRUST ME?"
W. T.

"CAN I USE YOUR TOILET PLEASE I'M BUSTING!"

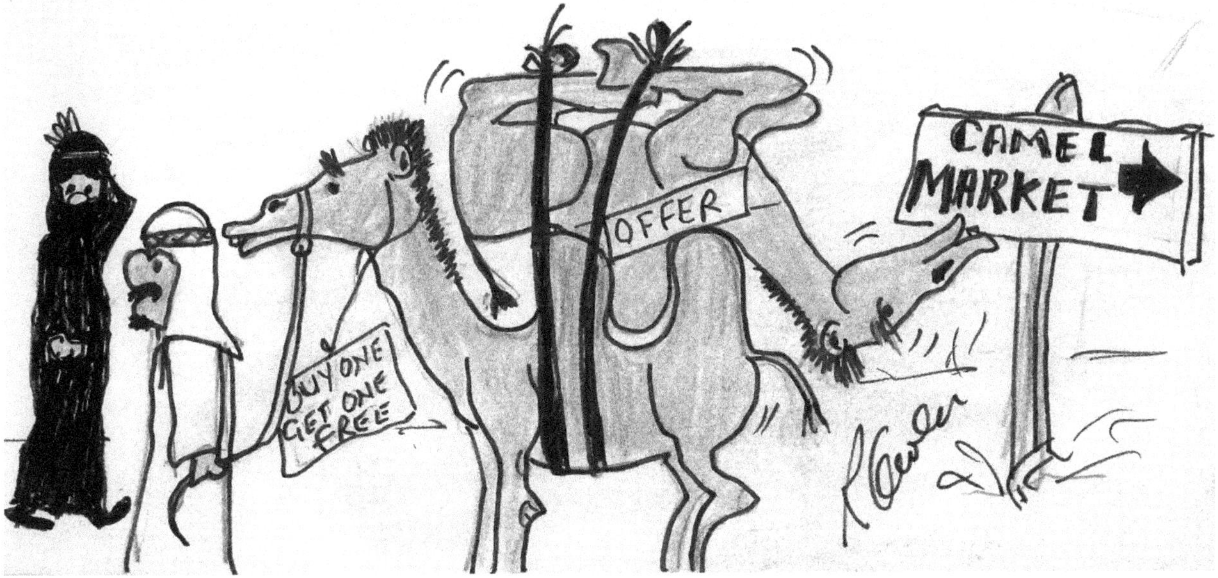
CAMEL MARKET
OFFER
BUY ONE GET ONE FREE

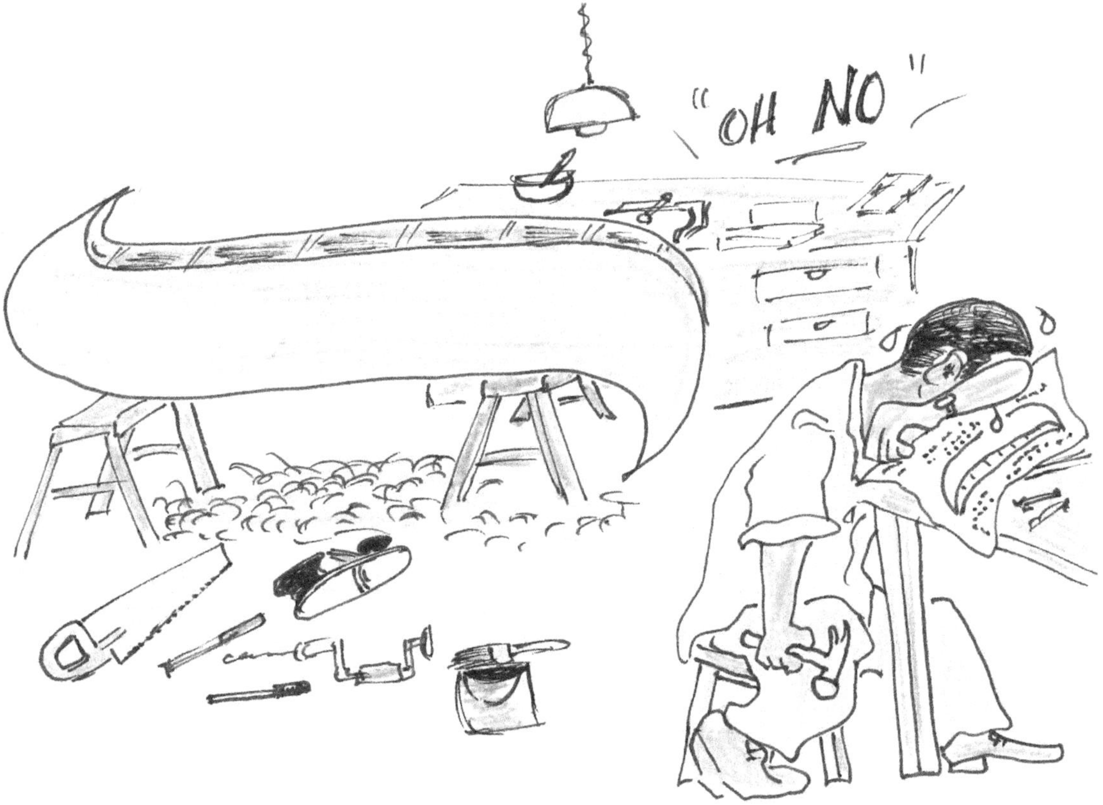
"OH NO"

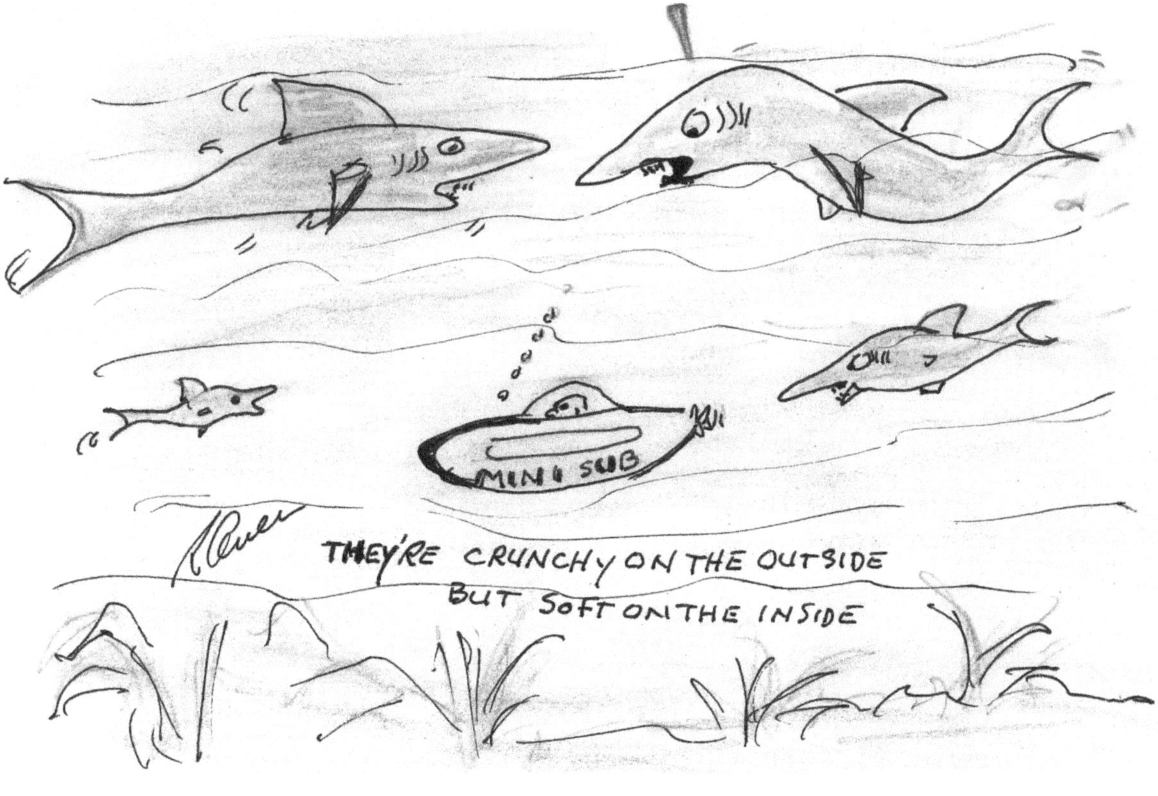
MINI SUB
THEY'RE CRUNCHY ON THE OUTSIDE
BUT SOFT ON THE INSIDE

"THE BUGGAR IS GOOD AT CATCHING THEM FROM MY POND!"

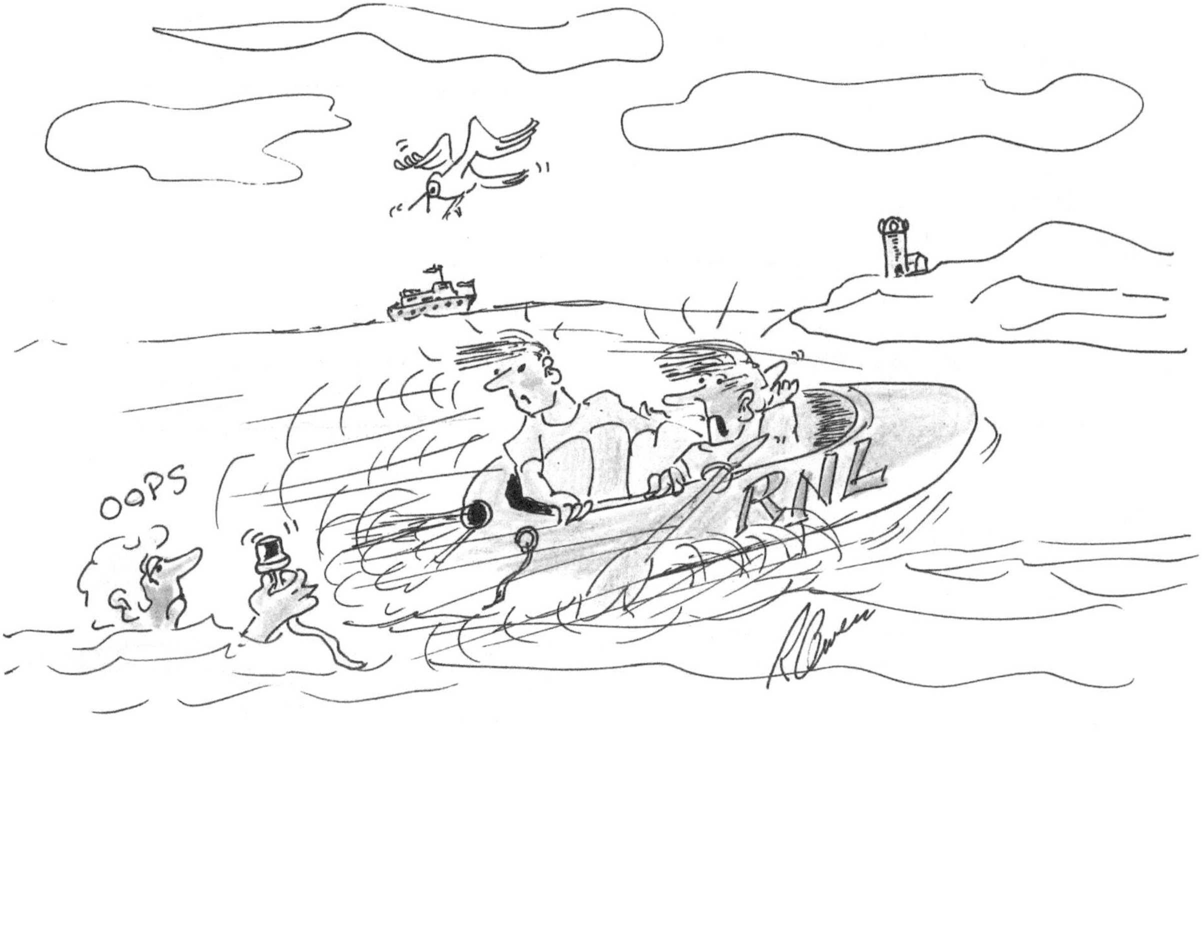
OOPS
RNL

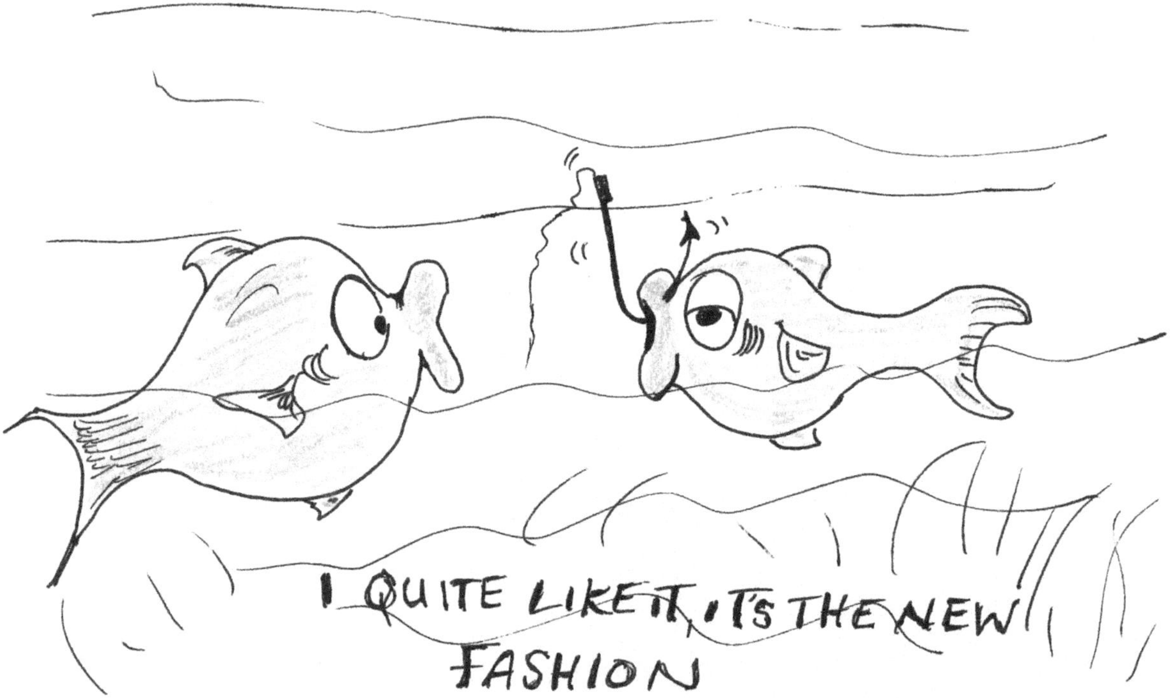
I QUITE LIKE IT, IT'S THE NEW FASHION

"I WOULDN'T IF I WERE YOU, MY BROTHER ATE ONE YESTERDAY AND VANISHED INTO THIN AIR!"

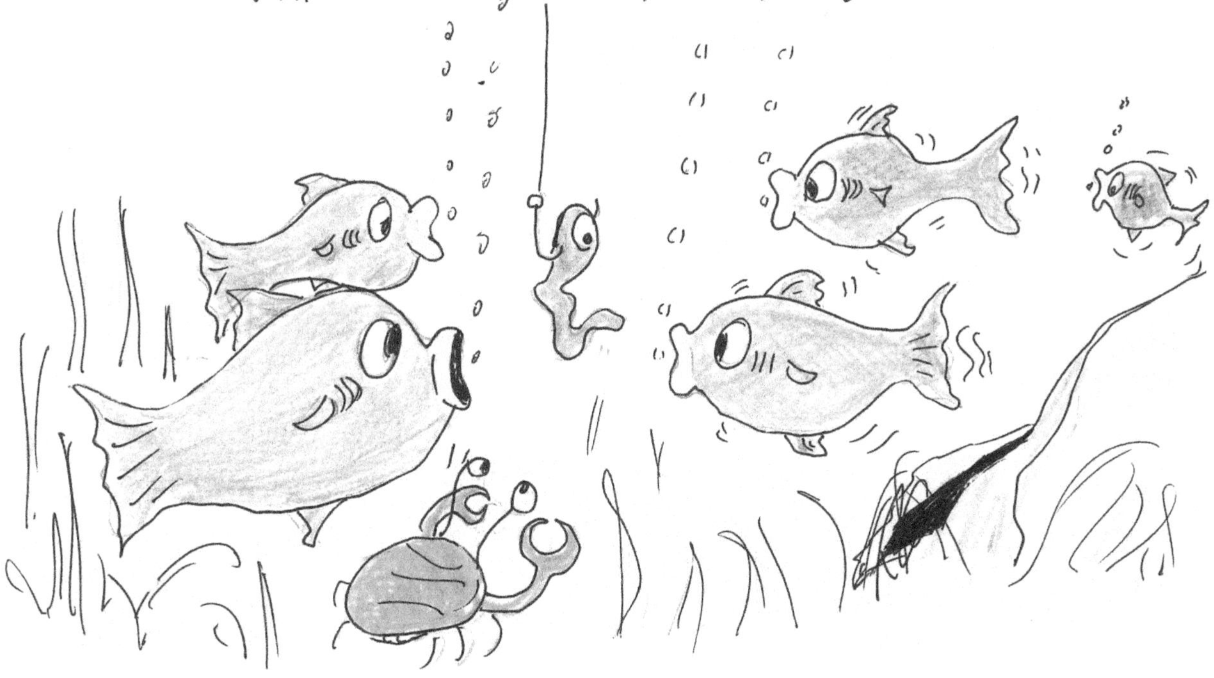

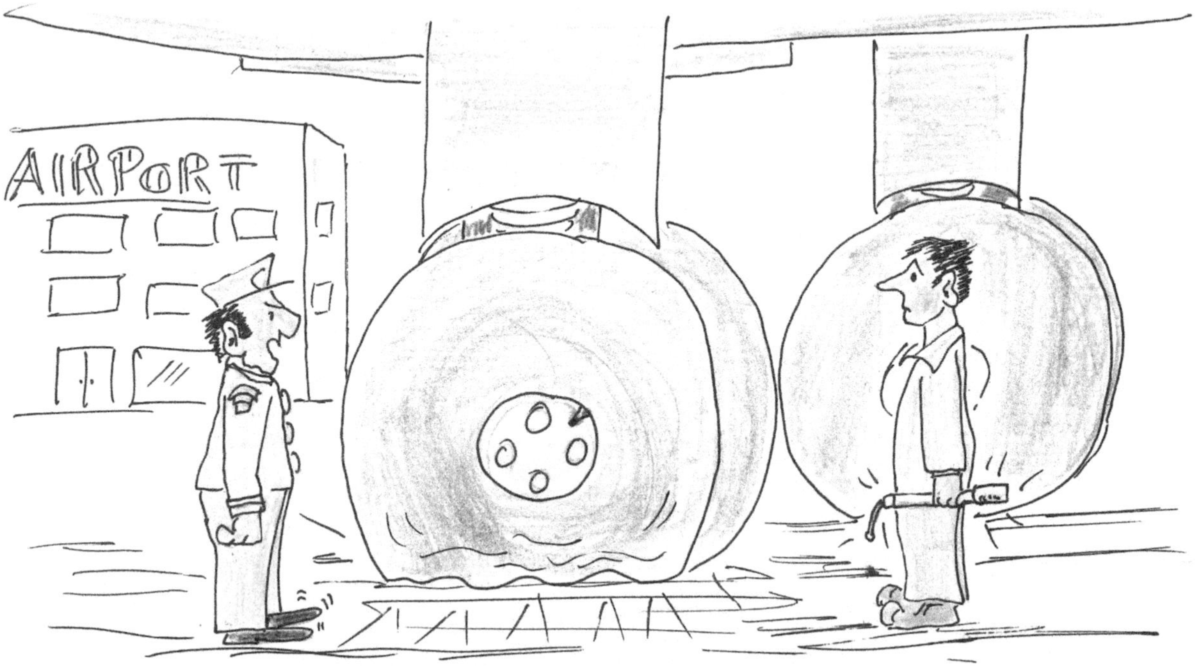
AIRPORT

"NEW AIN'T YOU?"

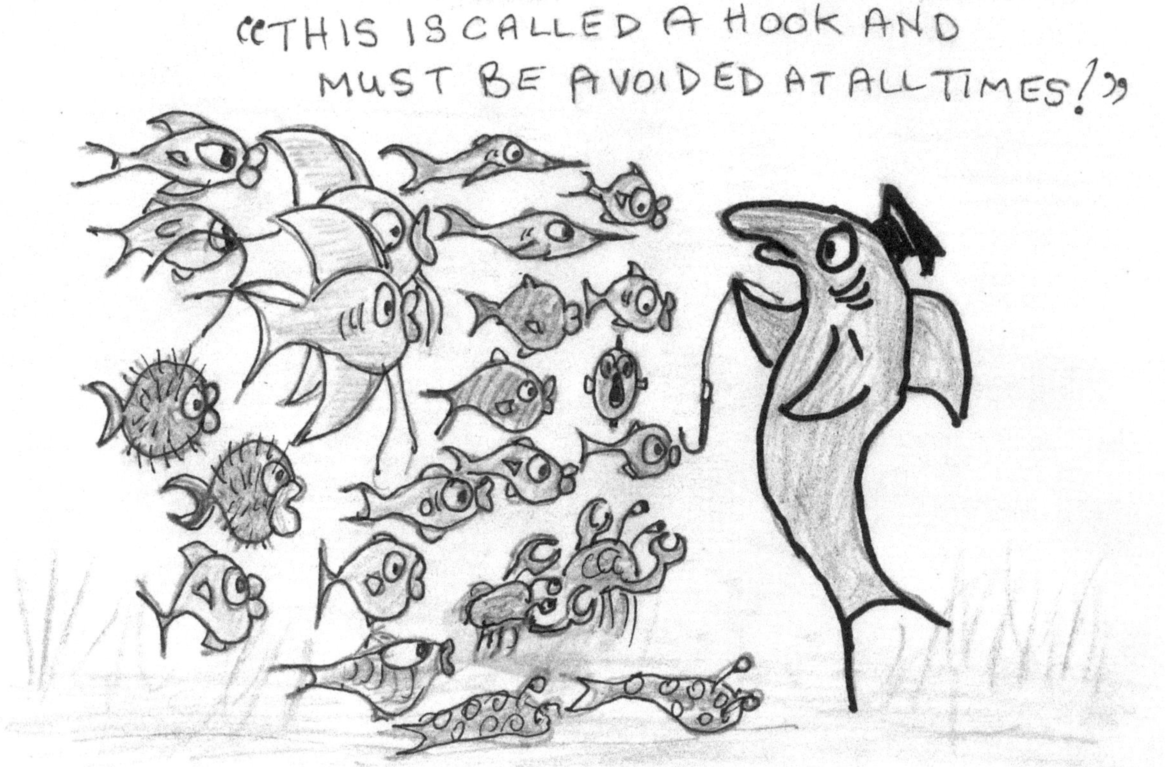
"THIS IS CALLED A HOOK AND
MUST BE AVOIDED AT ALL TIMES!"

"WATCH OUT FOR HIS LEFT HOOK!"

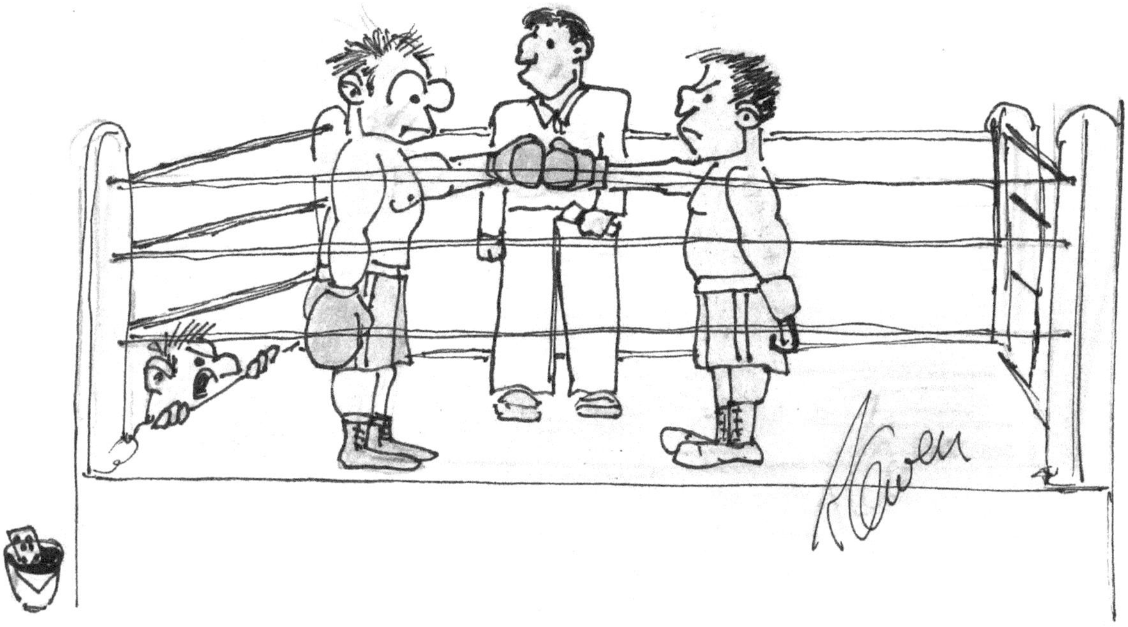

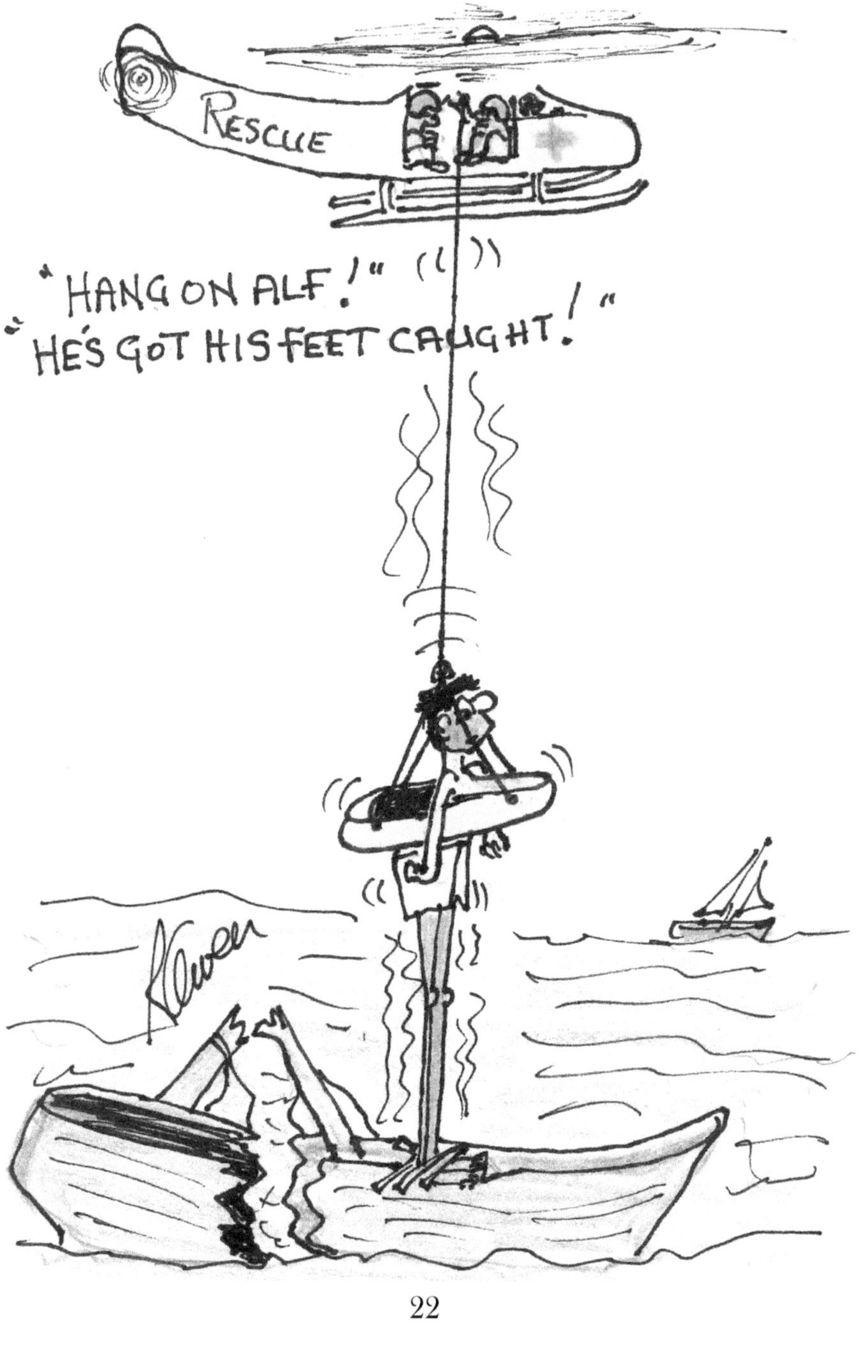
RESCUE
"HANG ON ALF!"
"HE'S GOT HIS FEET CAUGHT!"

"SORRY GRANDAD, YOU HAVE TO USE THE CARS WE PROVIDE!"

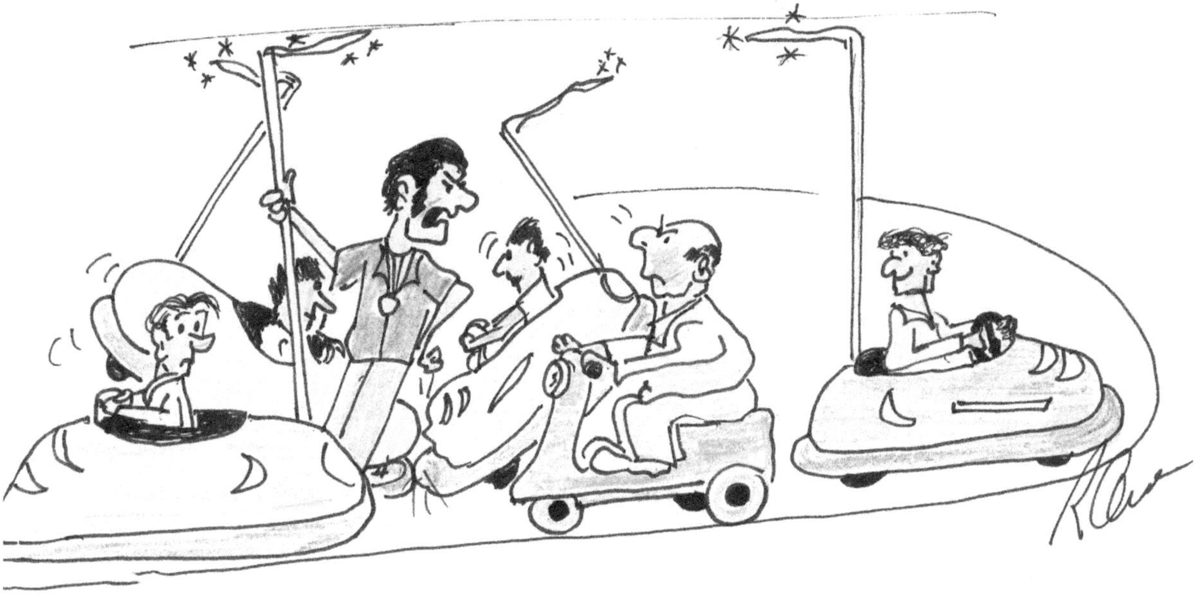

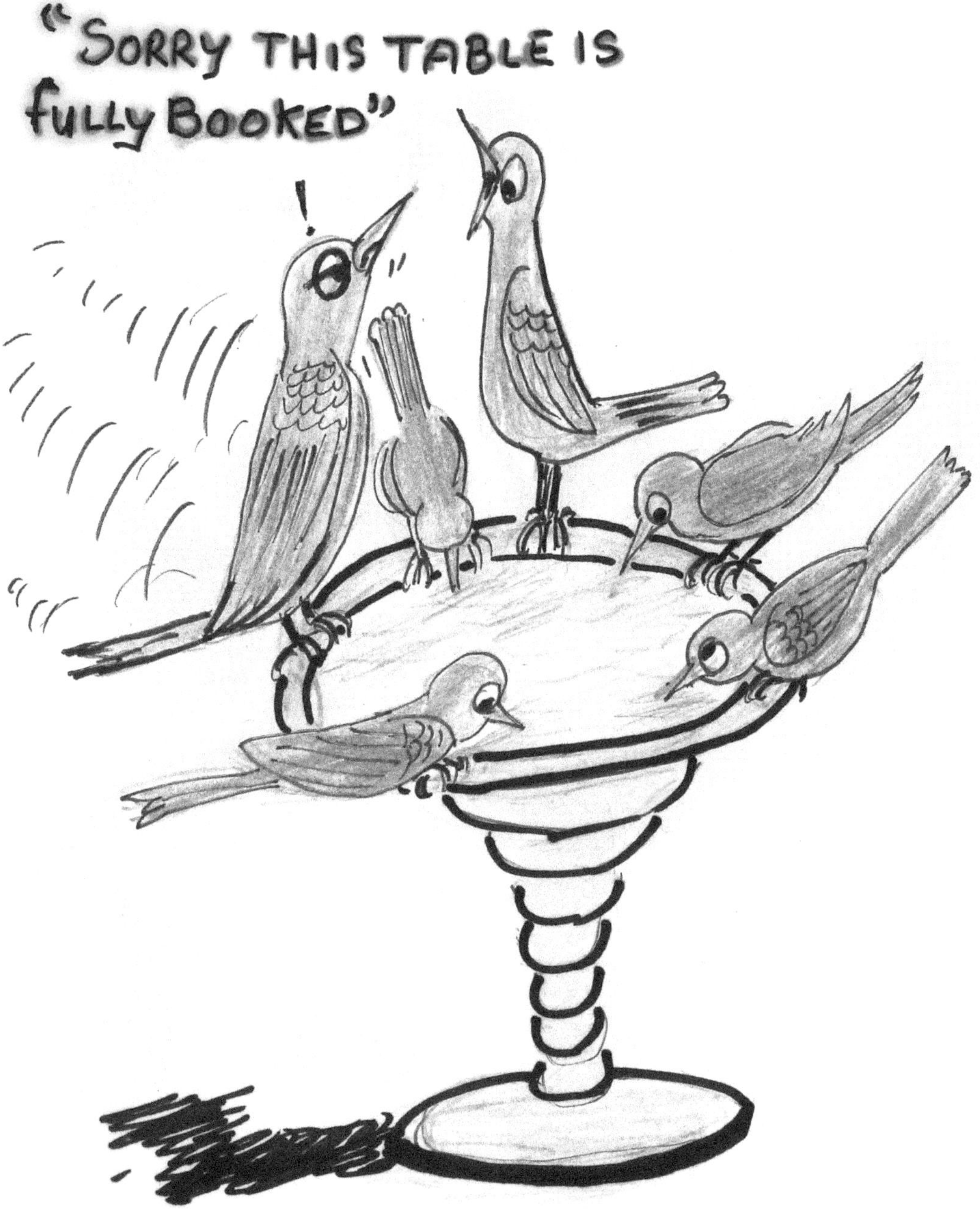
"SORRY THIS TABLE IS
FULLY BOOKED"
!

"WHAT HAVE I TOLD YOU, DON'T FEED THE FISH."

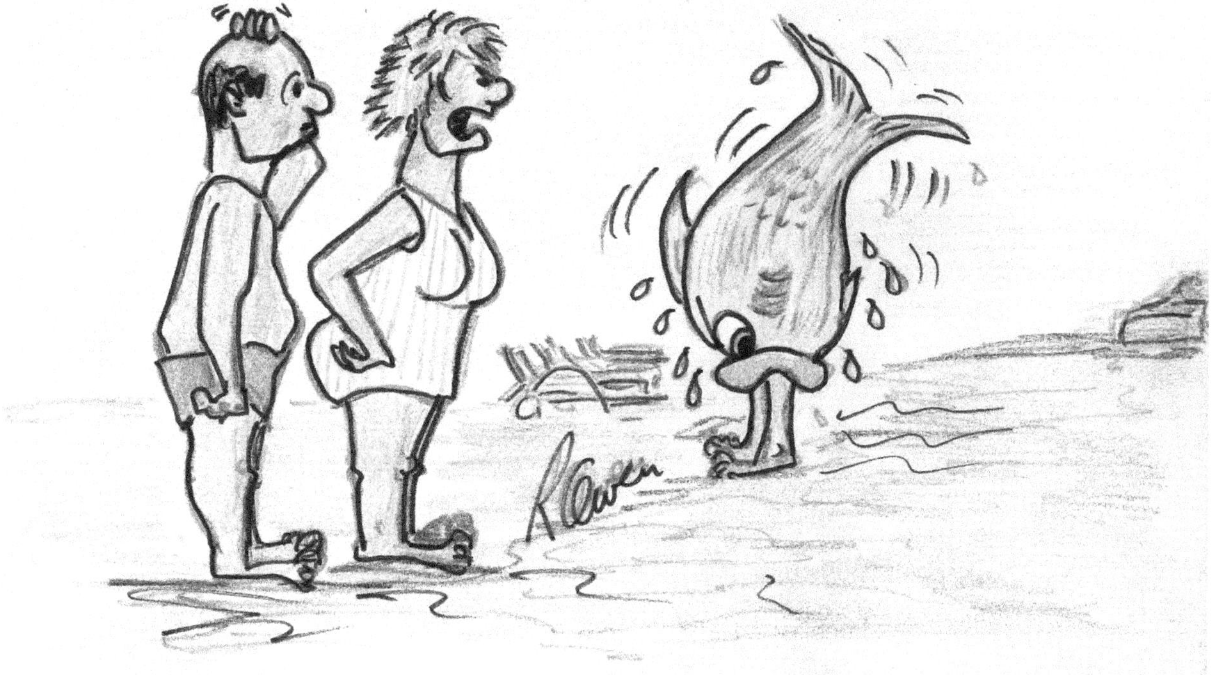

"HARRY I DON'T THINK THAT'S A DOLPHIN!"

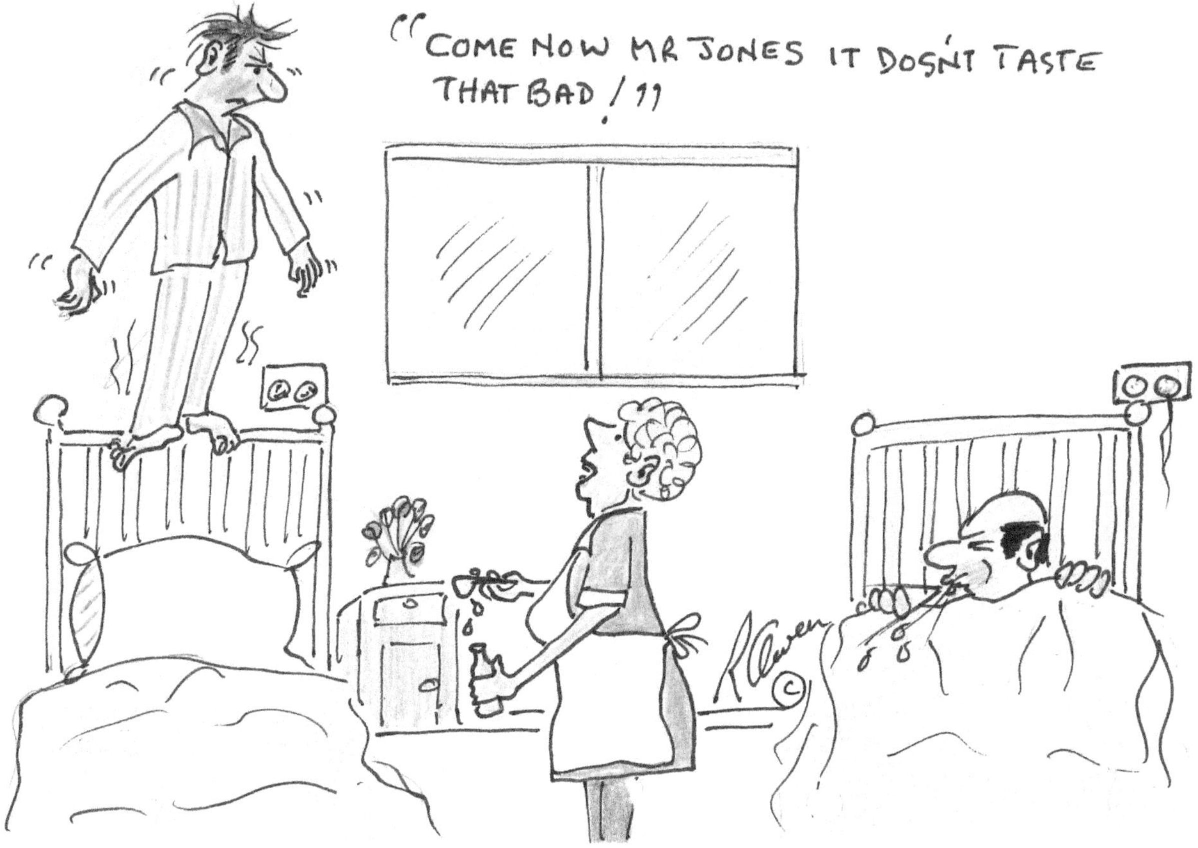
"COME NOW MR JONES IT DOSN'T TASTE THAT BAD!"

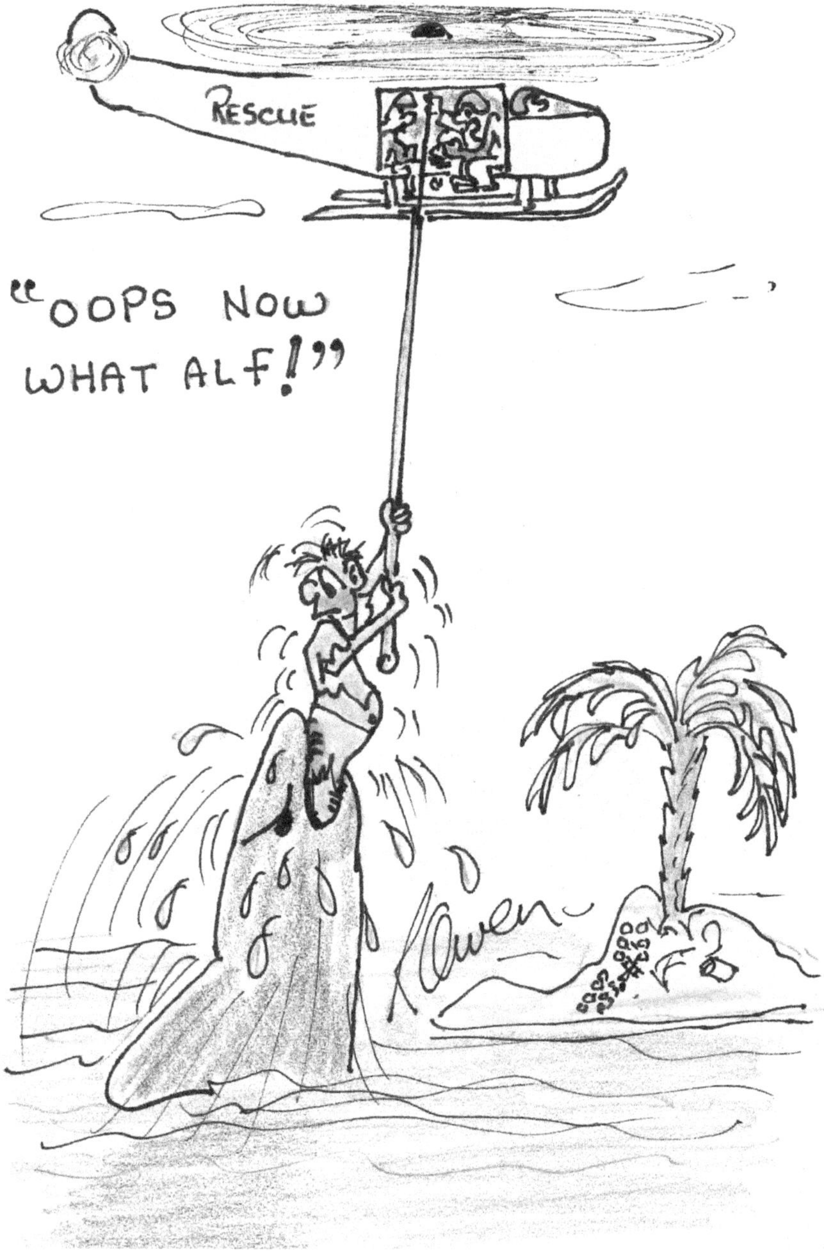
RESCUE
"OOPS NOW WHAT ALF!"
K Owen

"I CAN ASSURE YOU MADAM THE FONT IS NOT DEEP!"

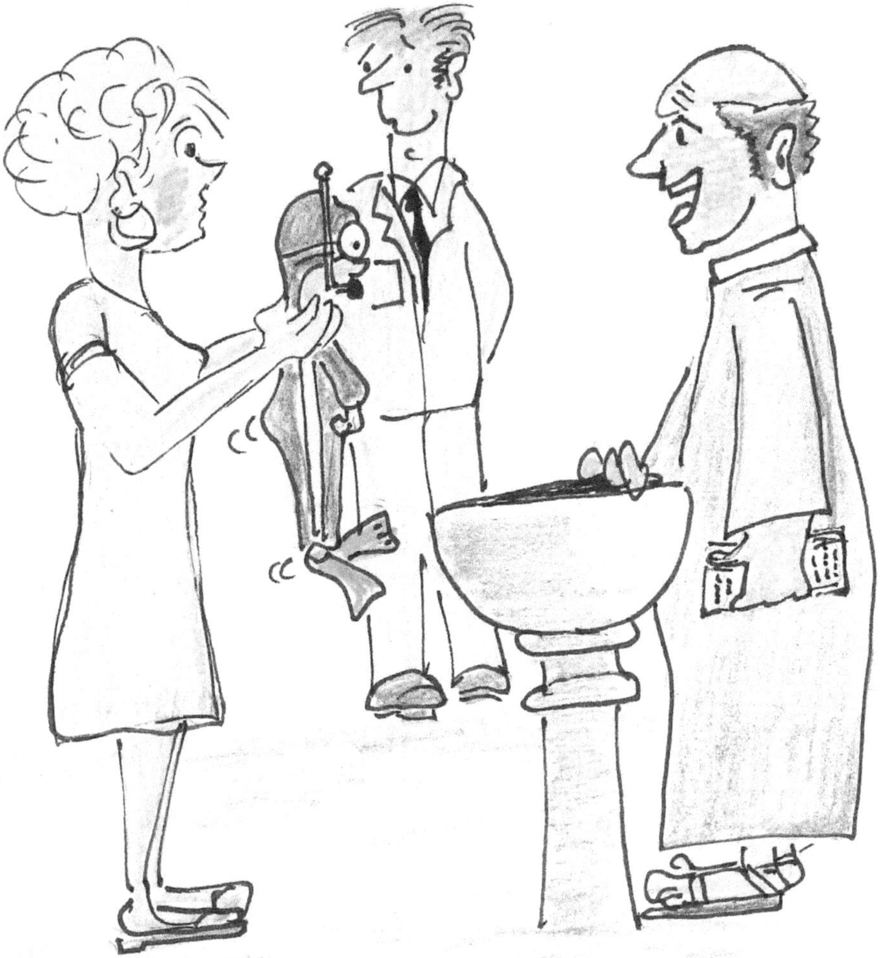

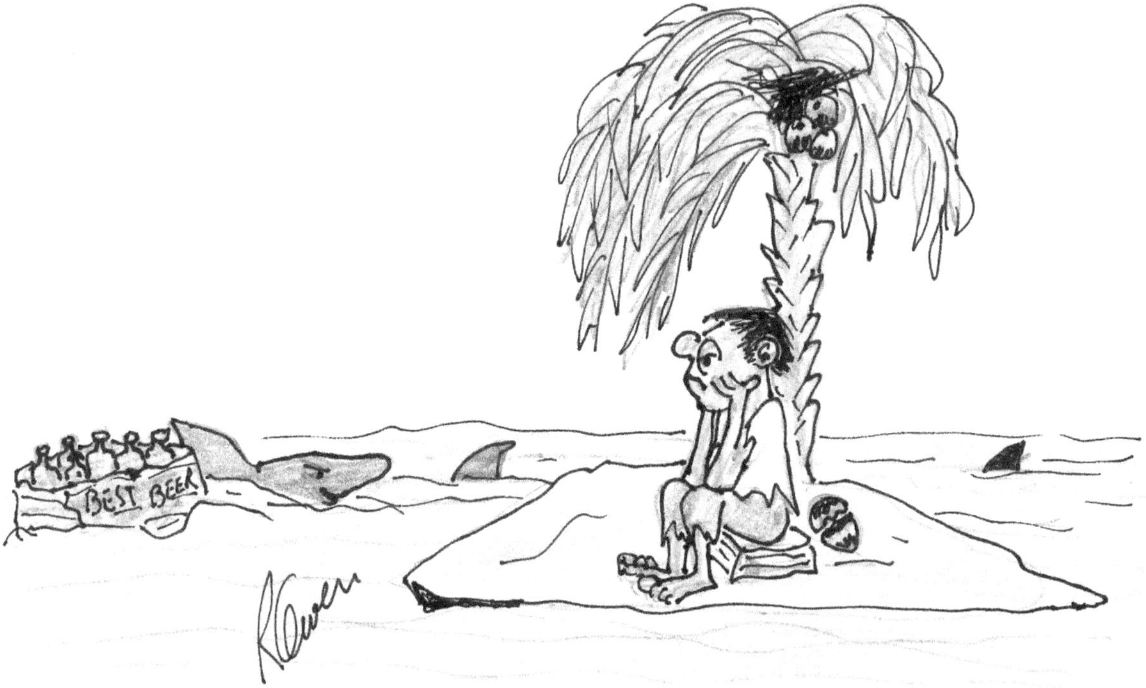
BEST BEER

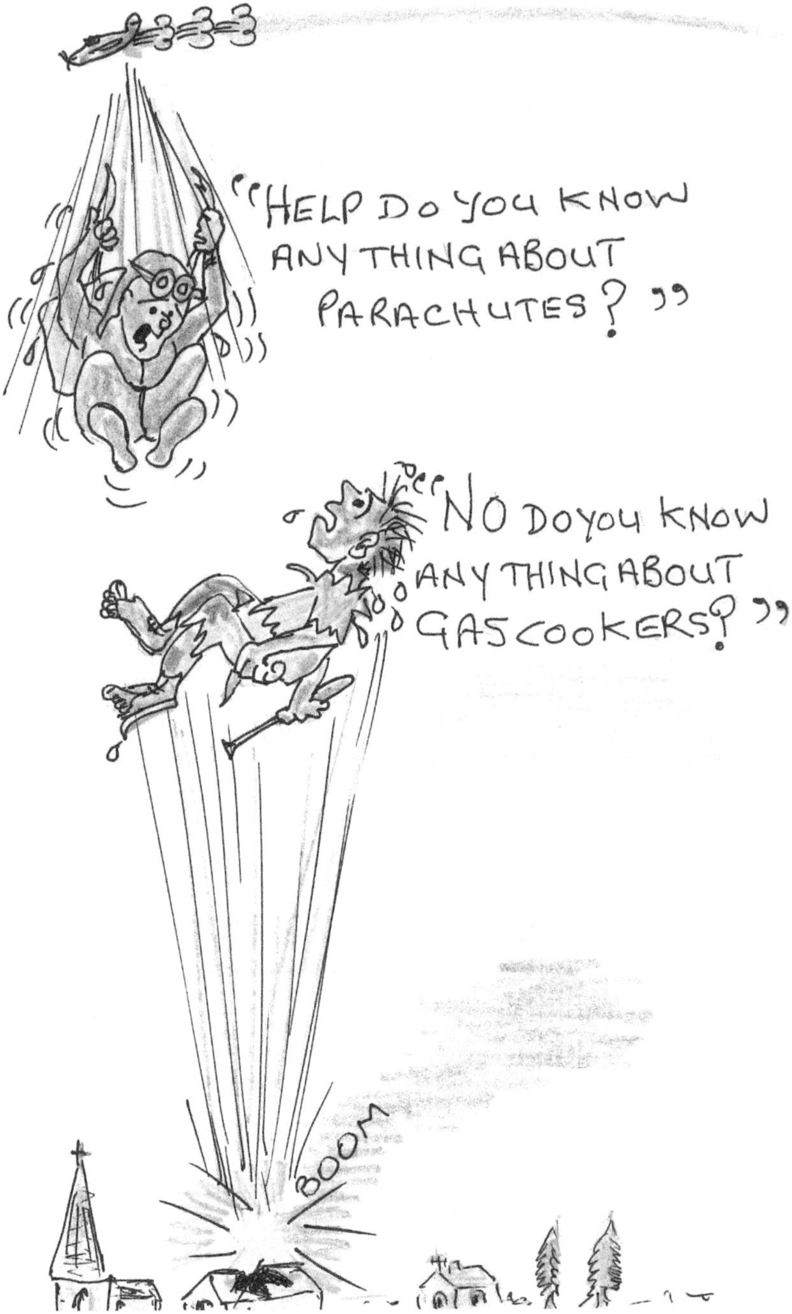
"HELP DO YOU KNOW ANY THING ABOUT PARACHUTES?"
"NO DO YOU KNOW ANY THING ABOUT GAS COOKERS?"
BOOM

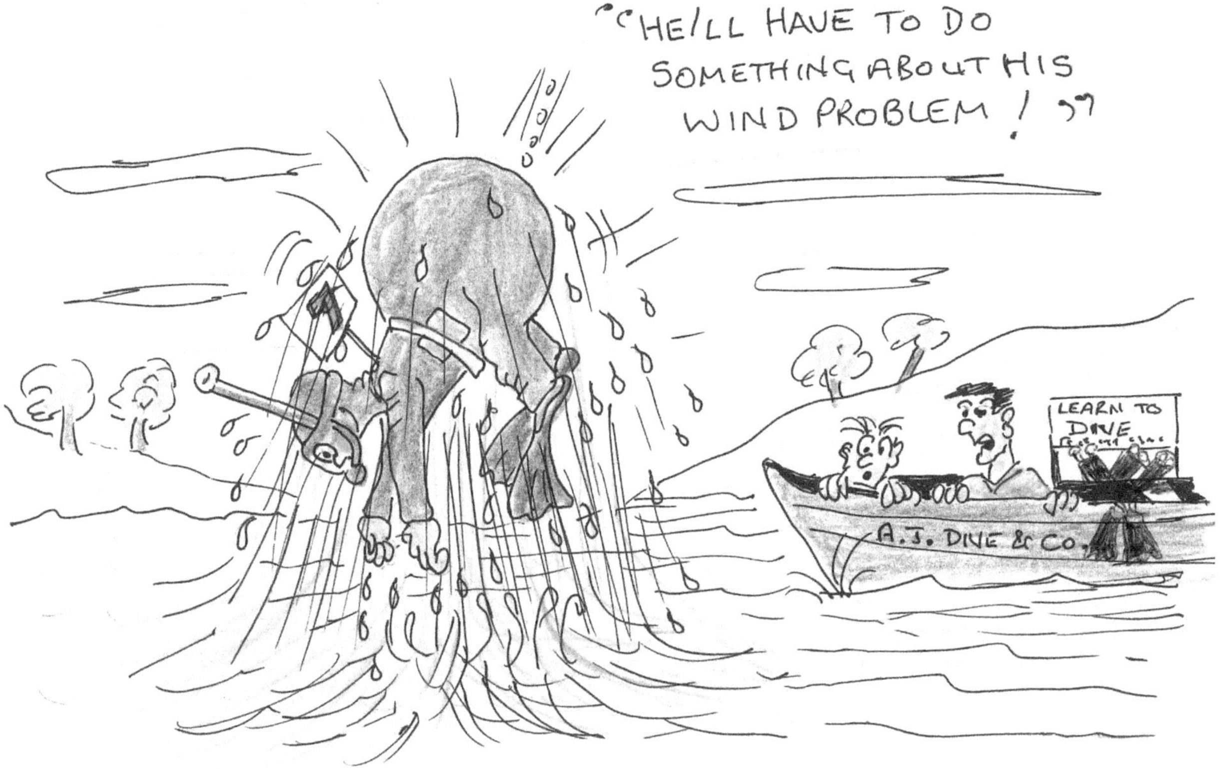
"HE'LL HAVE TO DO SOMETHING ABOUT HIS WIND PROBLEM!"
LEARN TO DIVE
A.J. DIVE & Co.

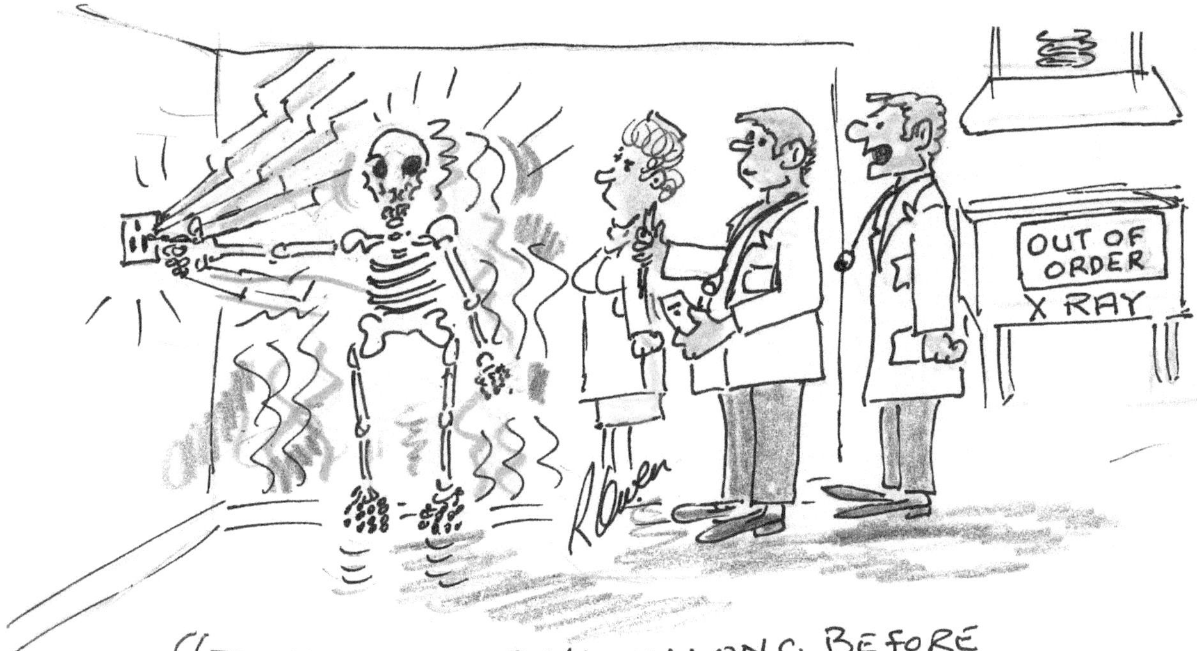
OUT OF ORDER
X RAY

"DID THEY SAY HOW LONG BEFORE THEY FIX THE REAL X RAY MACHINE!"

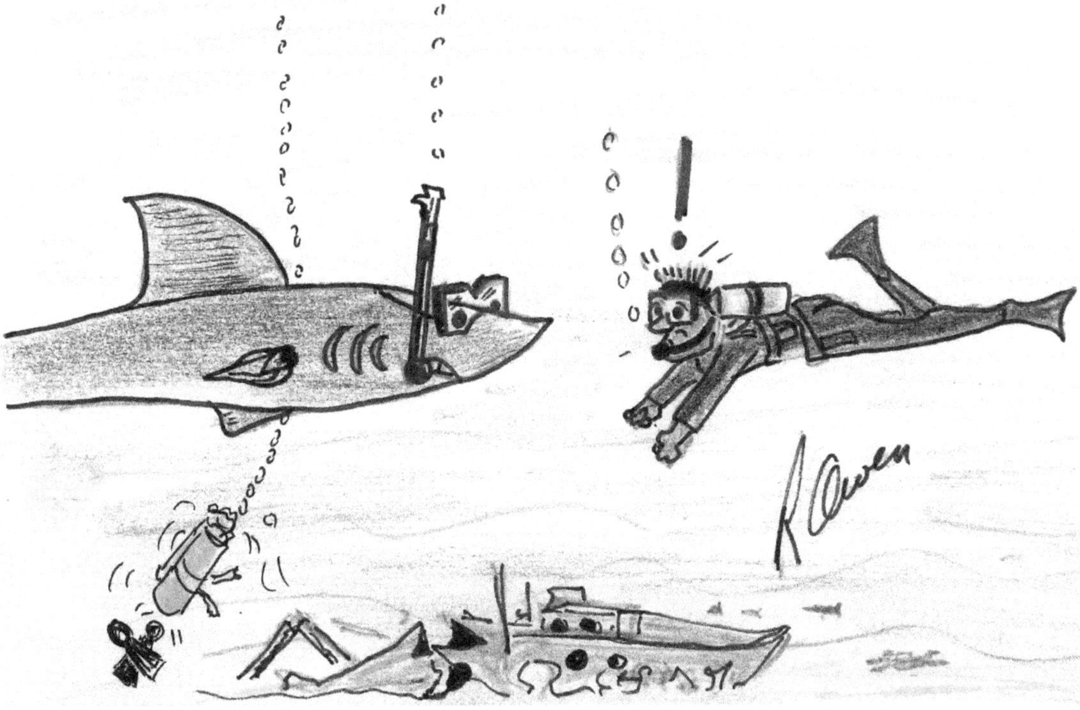
R Owen

"Sorry sir but there's a little delay with the squid!"

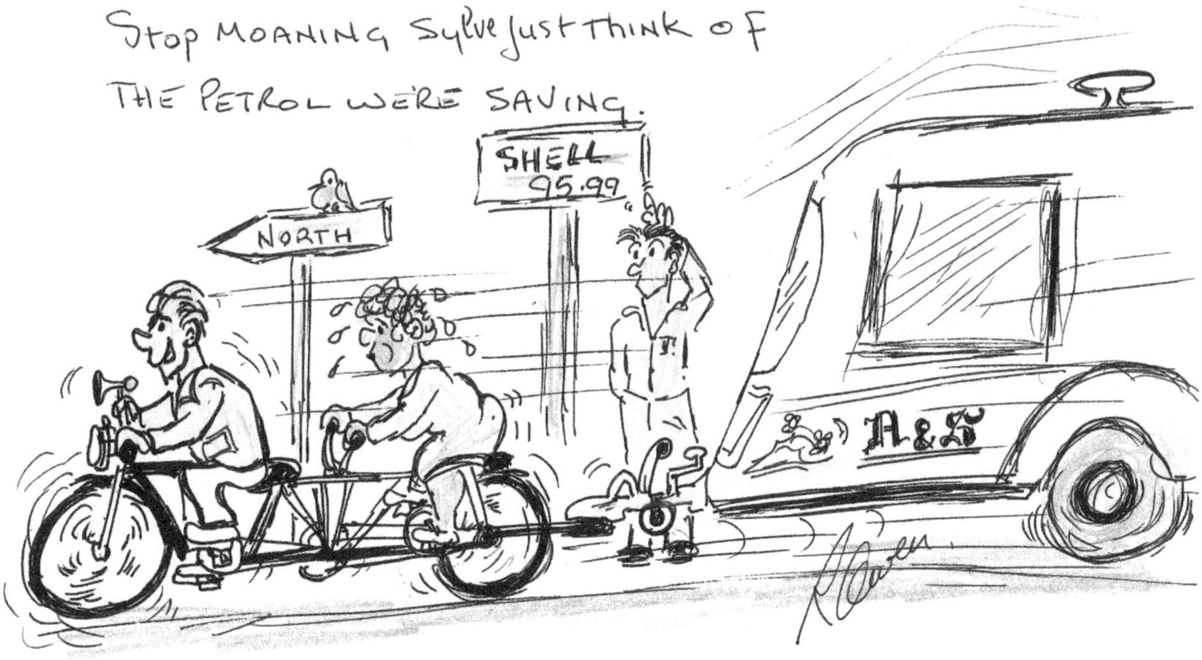
Stop MOANING Sylve just think of THE PETROL WE'RE SAVING.
NORTH
SHELL 95.99
A&S

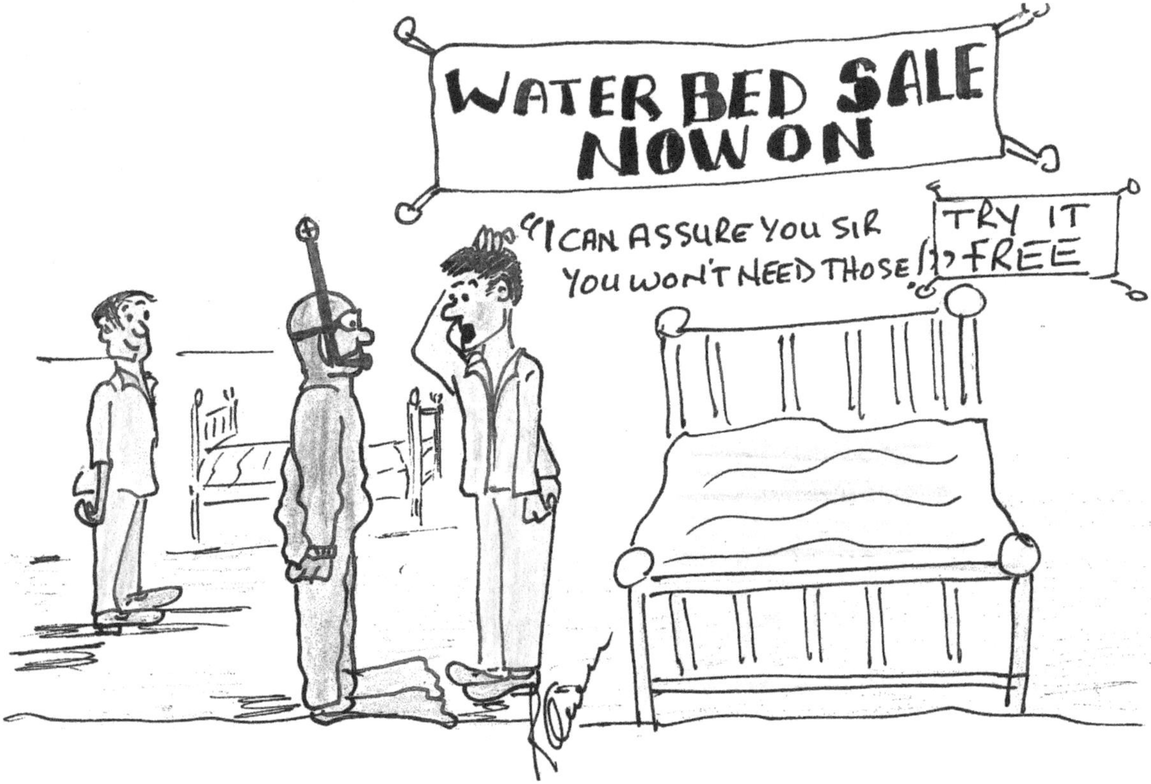
WATER BED SALE
NOW ON
"I CAN ASSURE YOU SIR
YOU WON'T NEED THOSE!!"
TRY IT
FREE

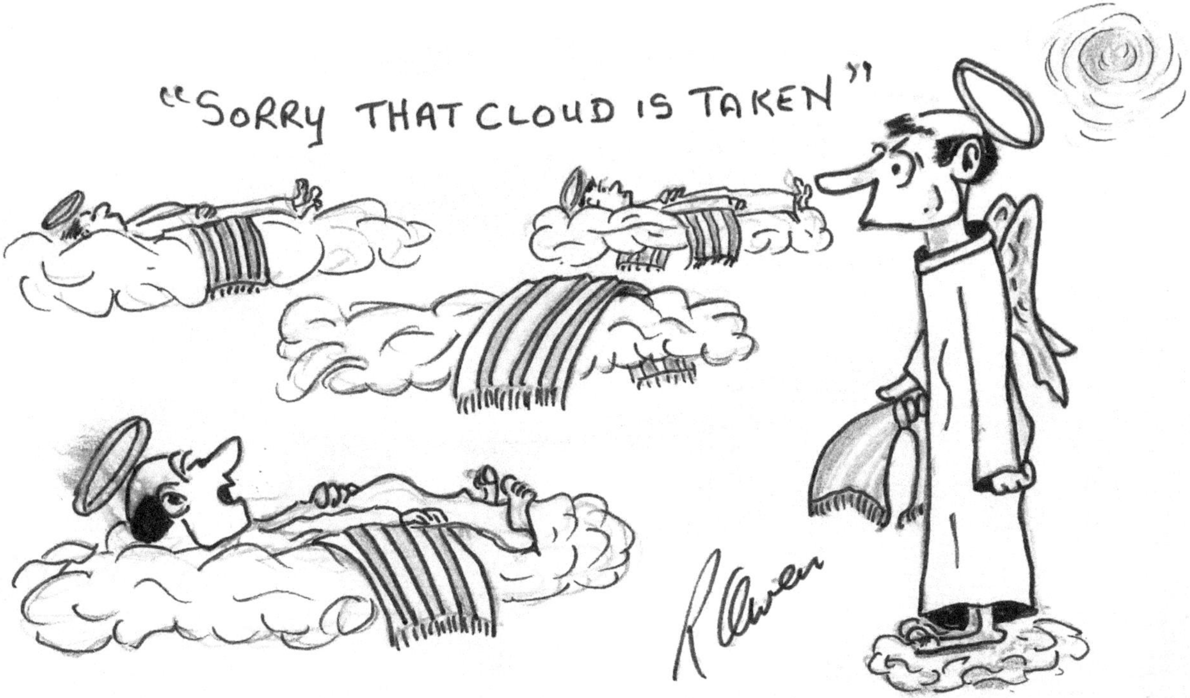
"SORRY THAT CLOUD IS TAKEN"
R Owen

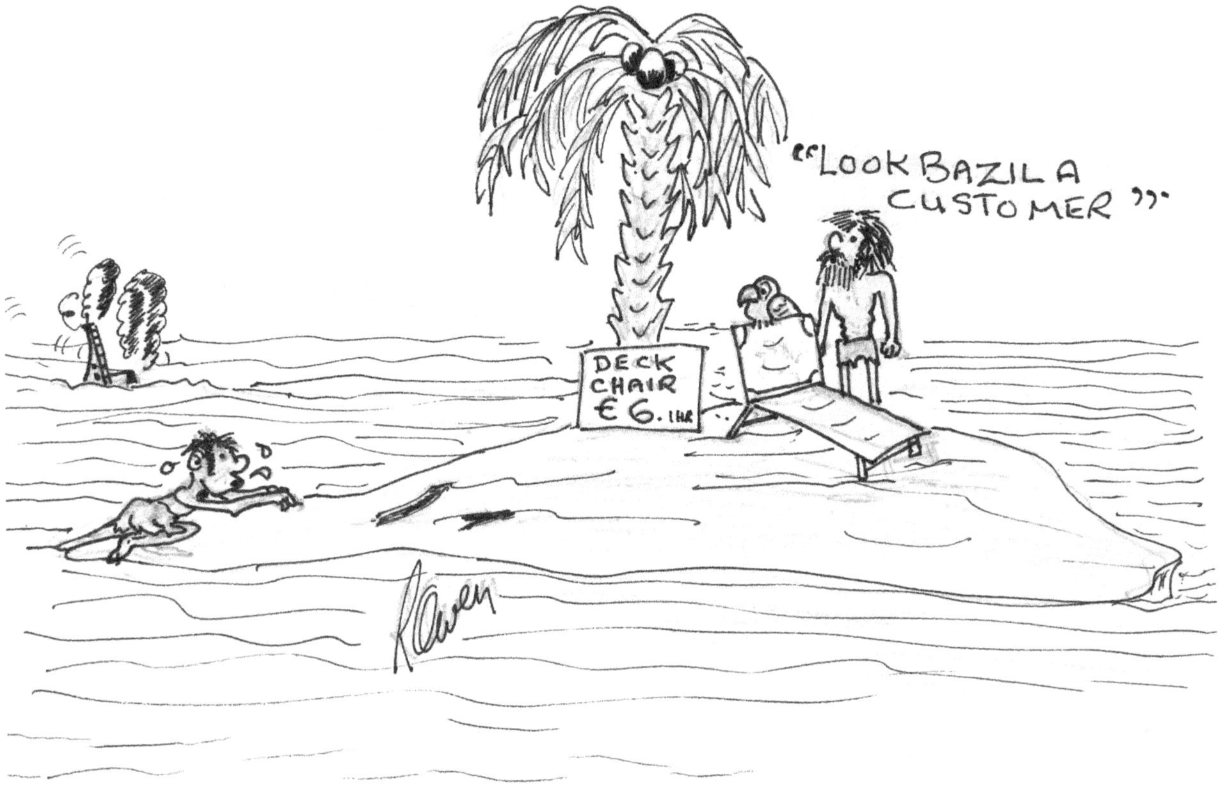
"LOOK BAZIL A CUSTOMER"
DECK CHAIR €6. 1HR

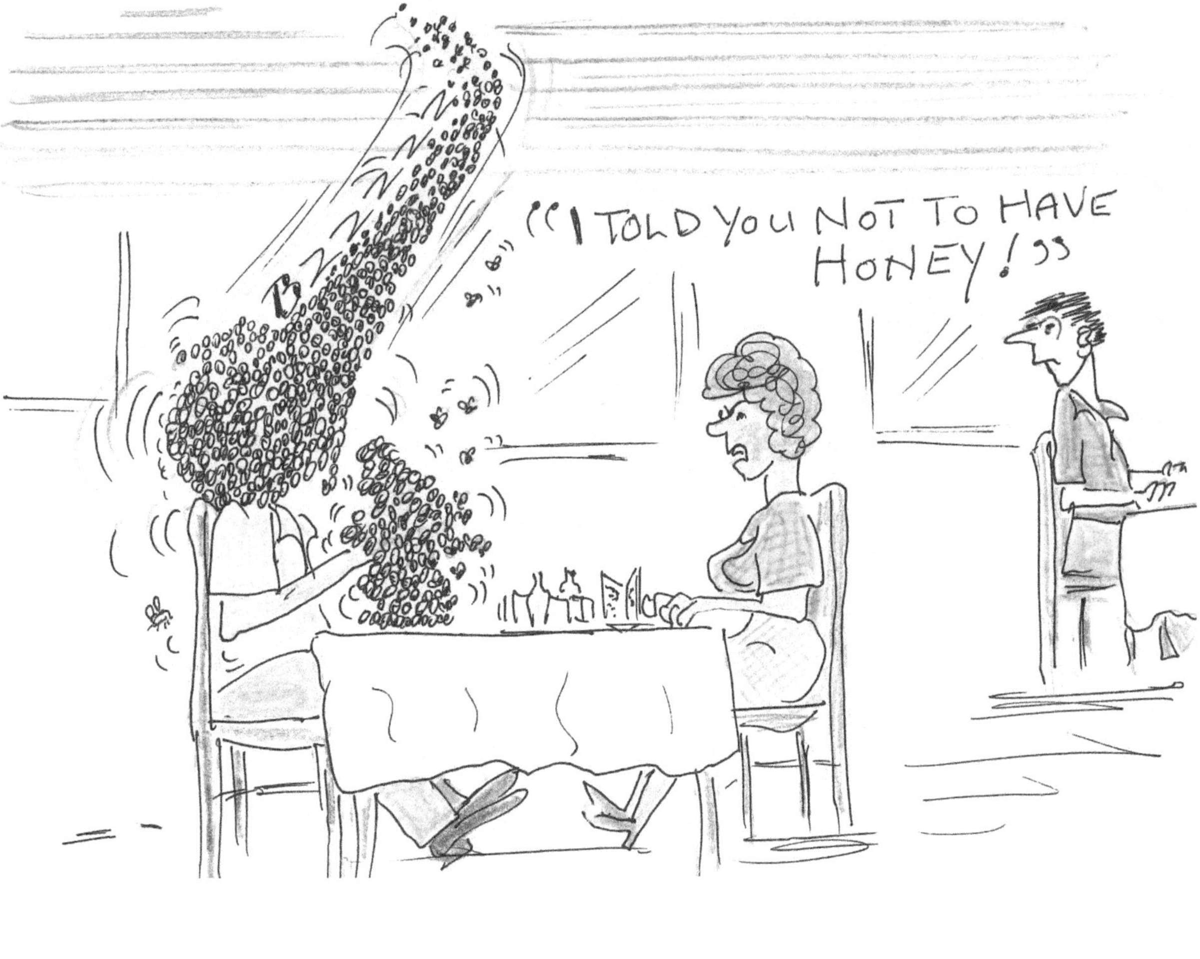
"I TOLD YOU NOT TO HAVE HONEY!"

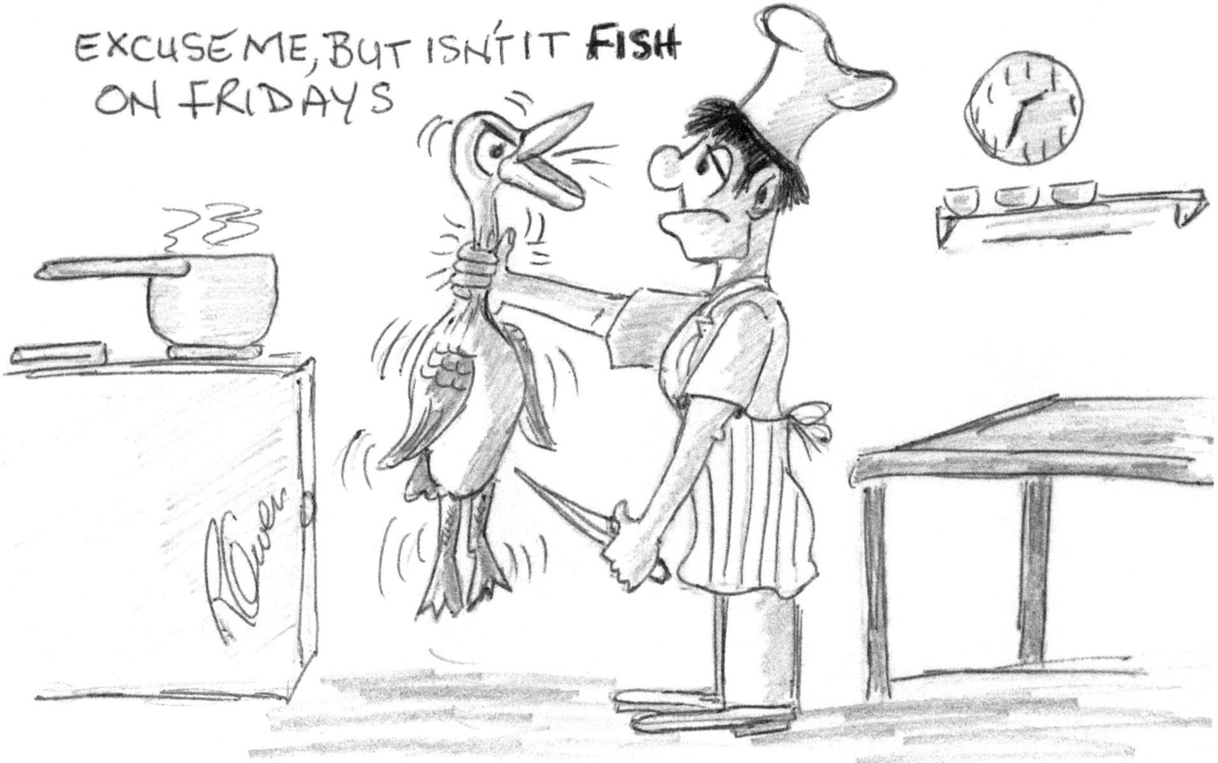
EXCUSE ME, BUT ISN'T IT FISH ON FRIDAYS

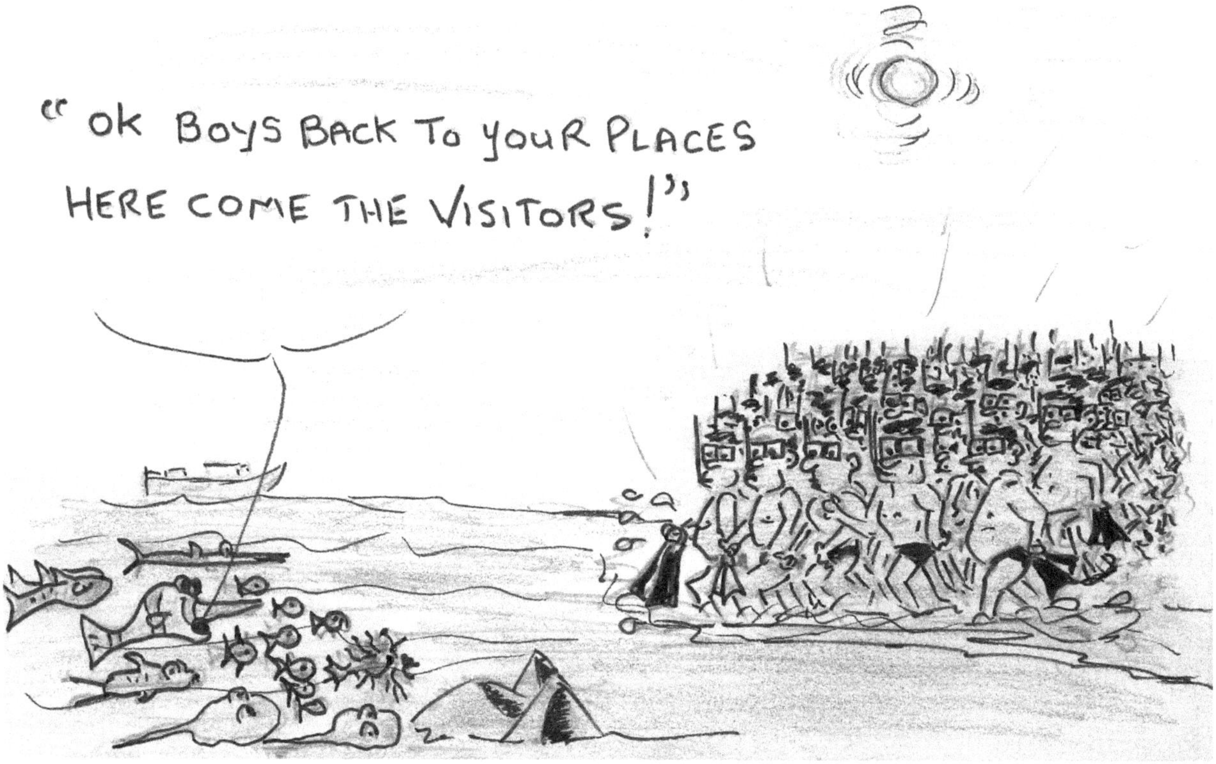
"OK BOYS BACK TO YOUR PLACES
HERE COME THE VISITORS!"

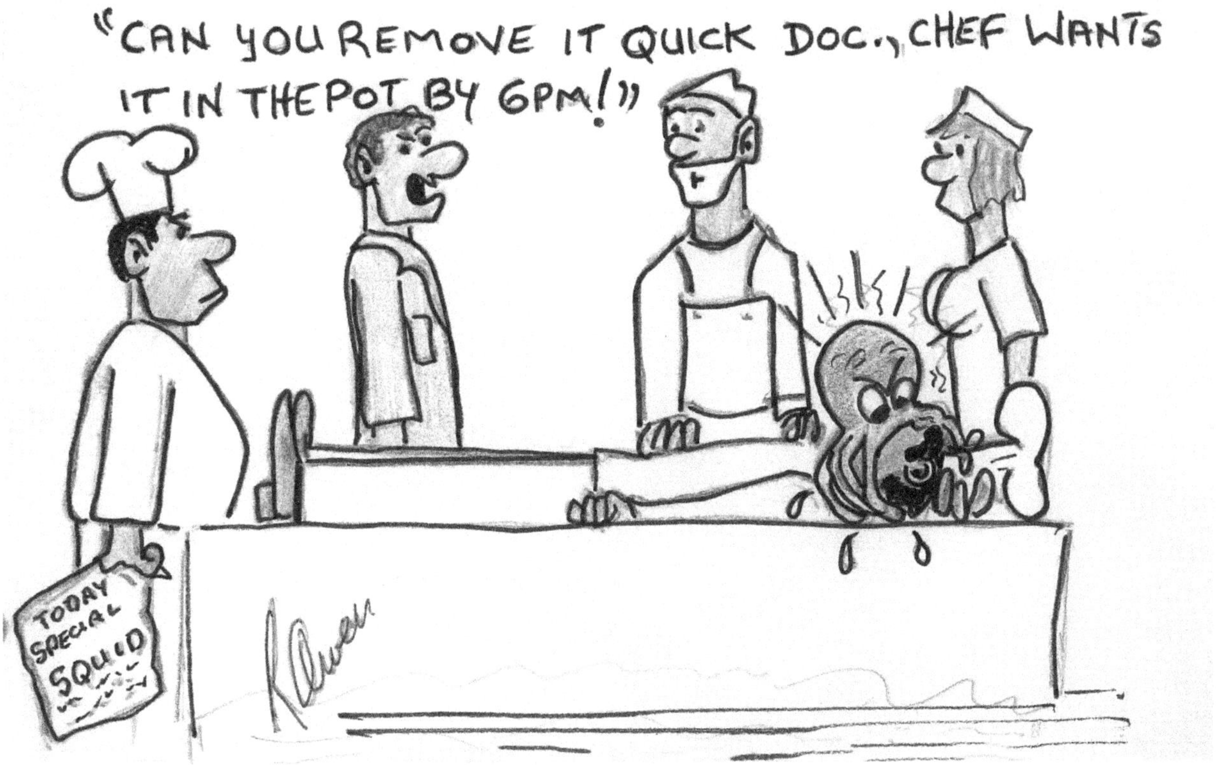
"CAN YOU REMOVE IT QUICK DOC., CHEF WANTS IT IN THE POT BY 6PM!"
TODAY SPECIAL SQUID

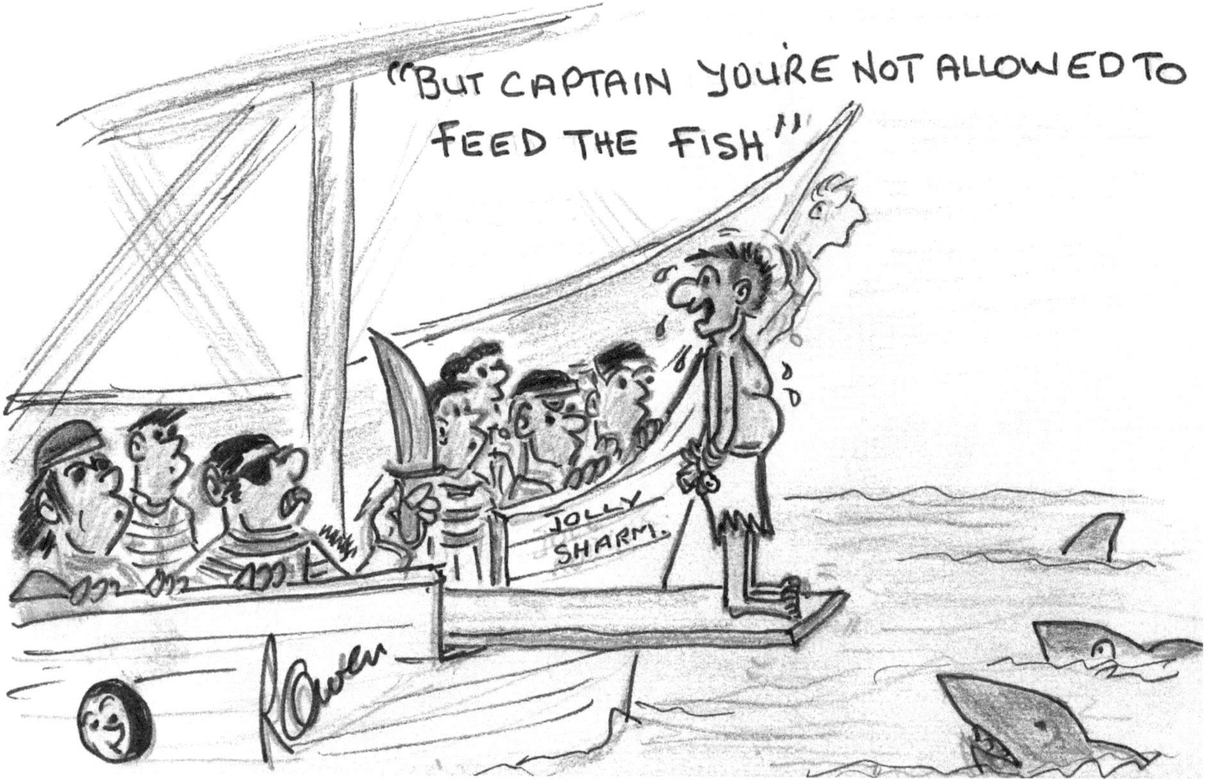
"BUT CAPTAIN YOU'RE NOT ALLOWED TO FEED THE FISH"
JOLLY SHARM.

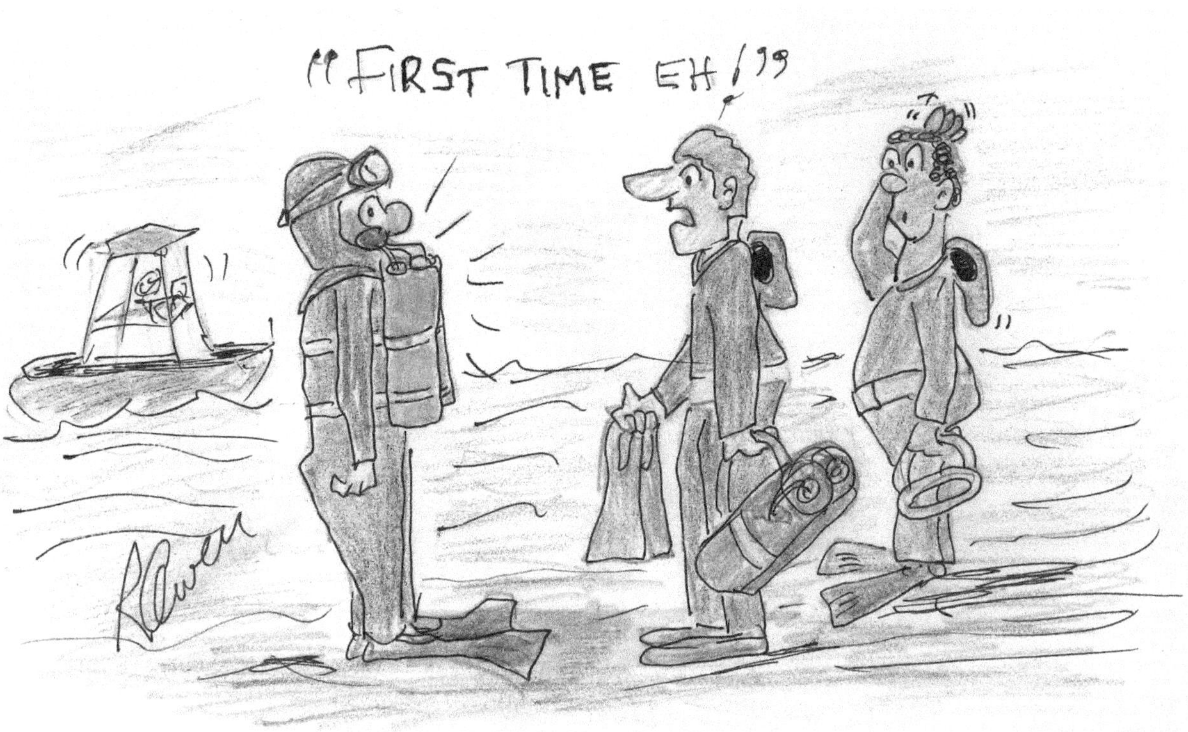
"FIRST TIME EH!"

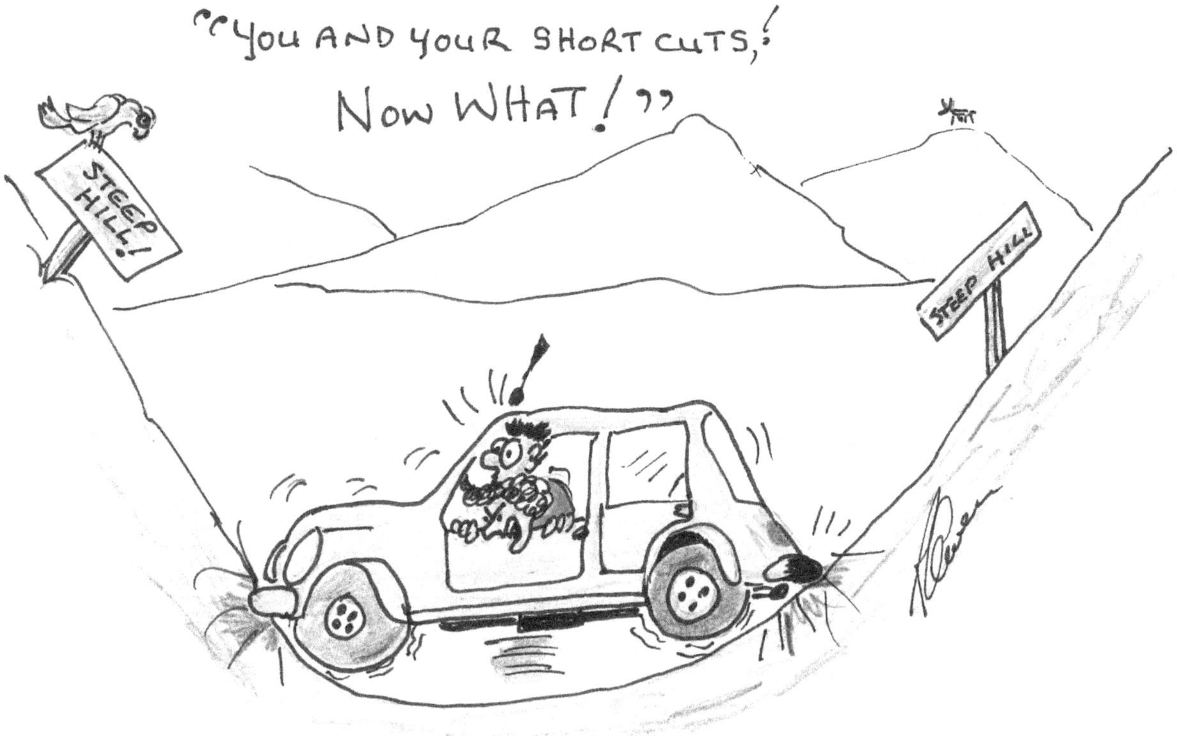
"YOU AND YOUR SHORT CUTS,!
NOW WHAT!"
STEEP HILL!
STEEP HILL

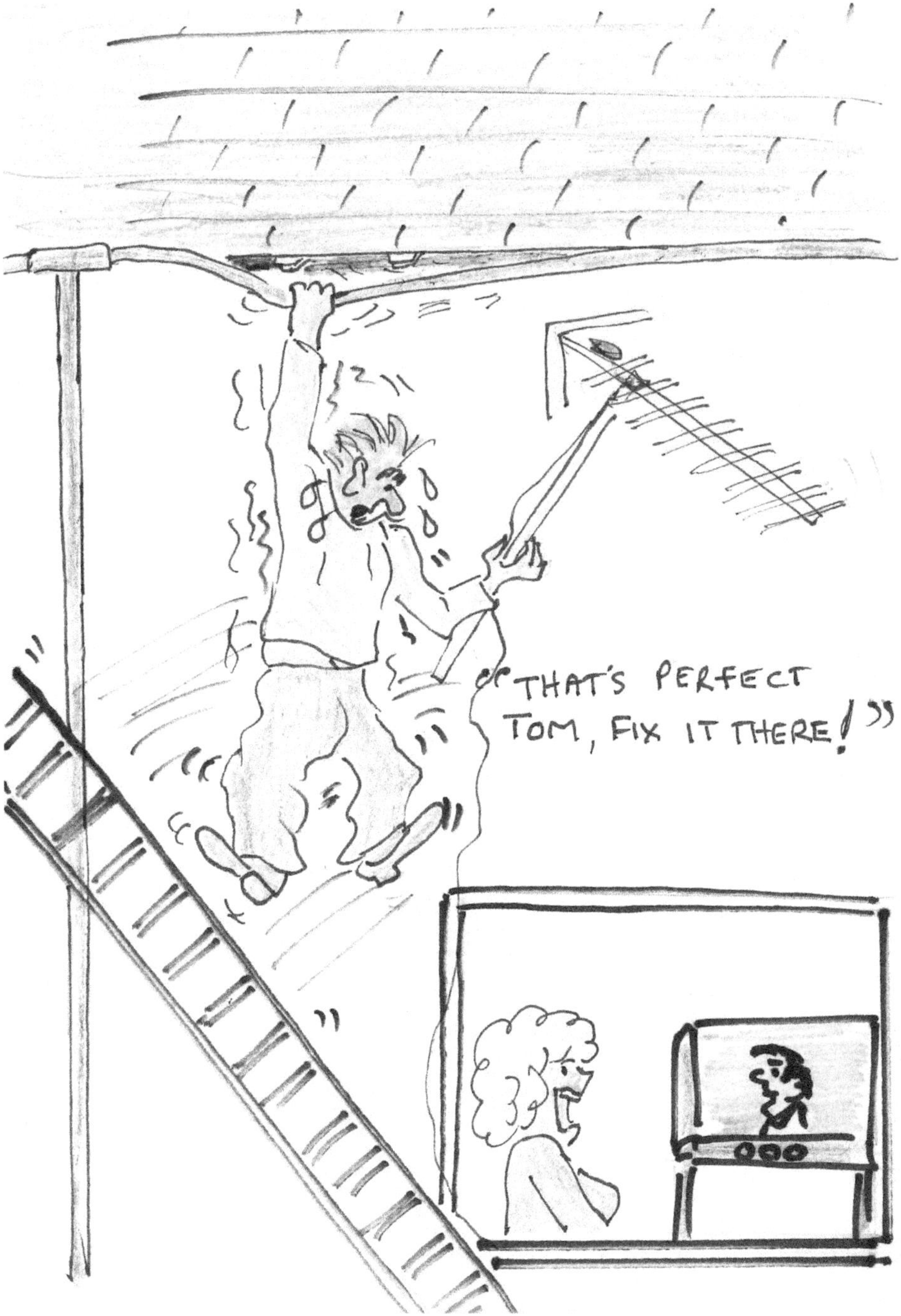
"THAT'S PERFECT TOM, FIX IT THERE!"

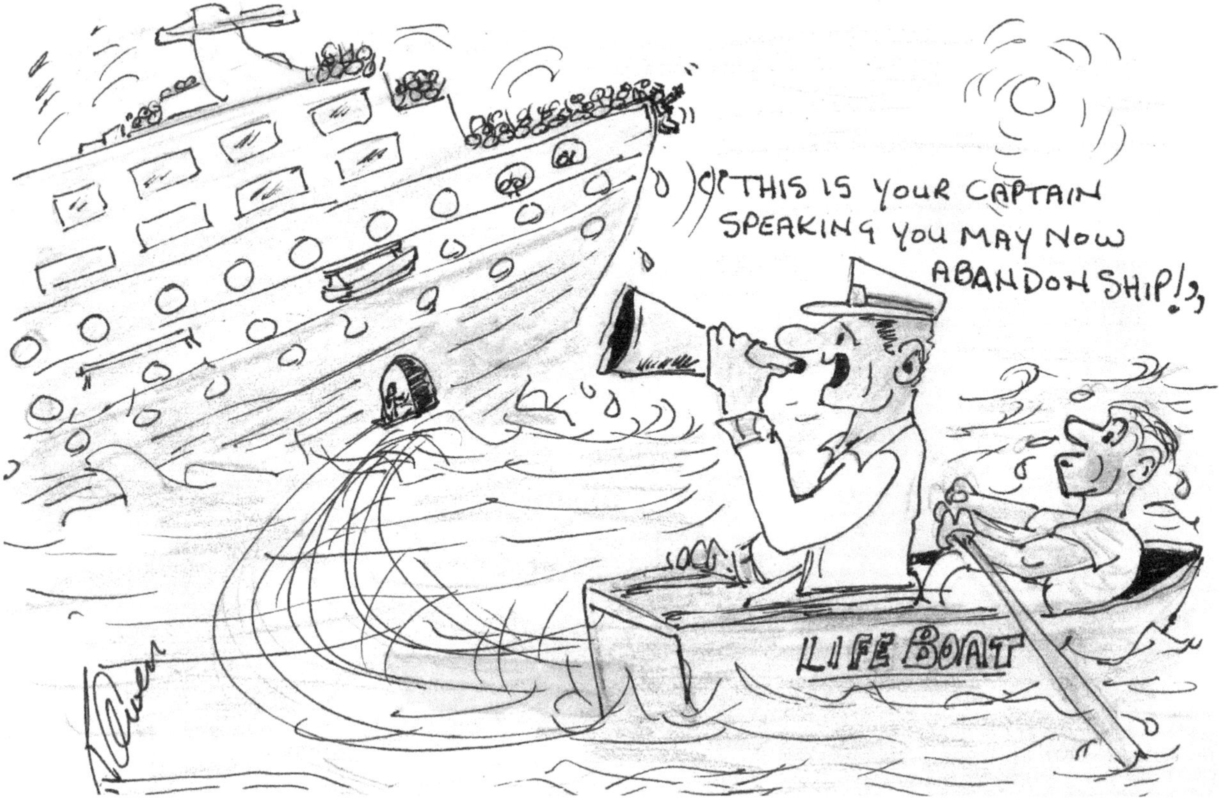
"THIS IS YOUR CAPTAIN SPEAKING YOU MAY NOW ABANDON SHIP!"
LIFE BOAT

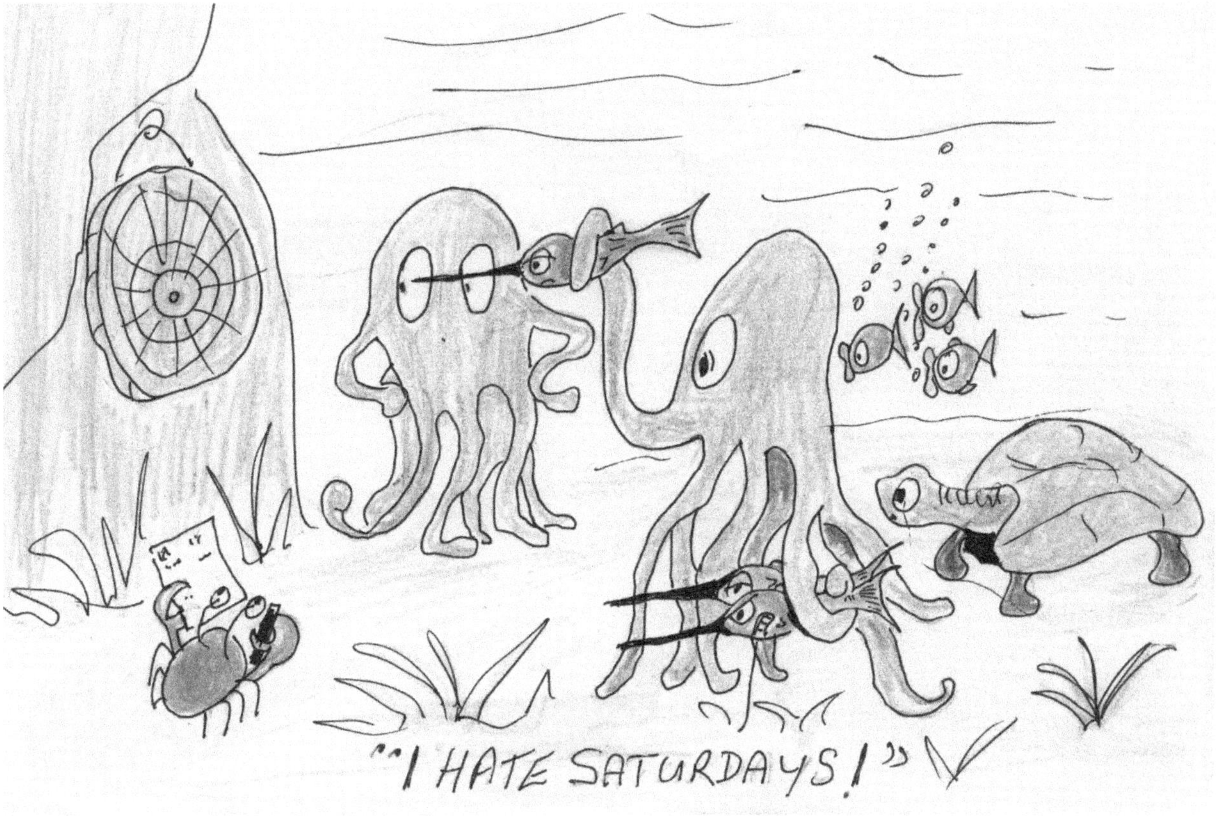
"I HATE SATURDAYS!"

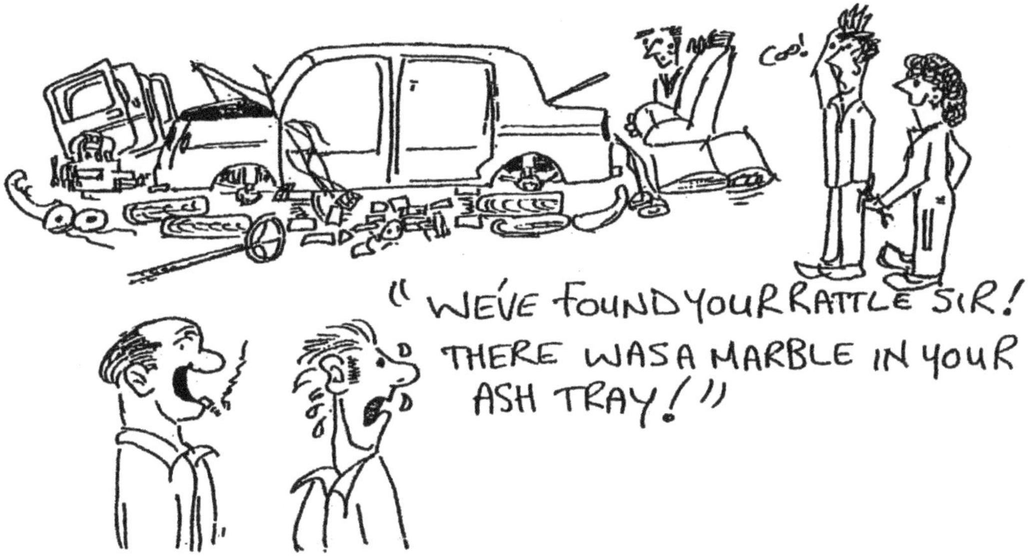
COO!
" WE'VE FOUND YOUR RATTLE SIR!
THERE WAS A MARBLE IN YOUR
ASH TRAY! "

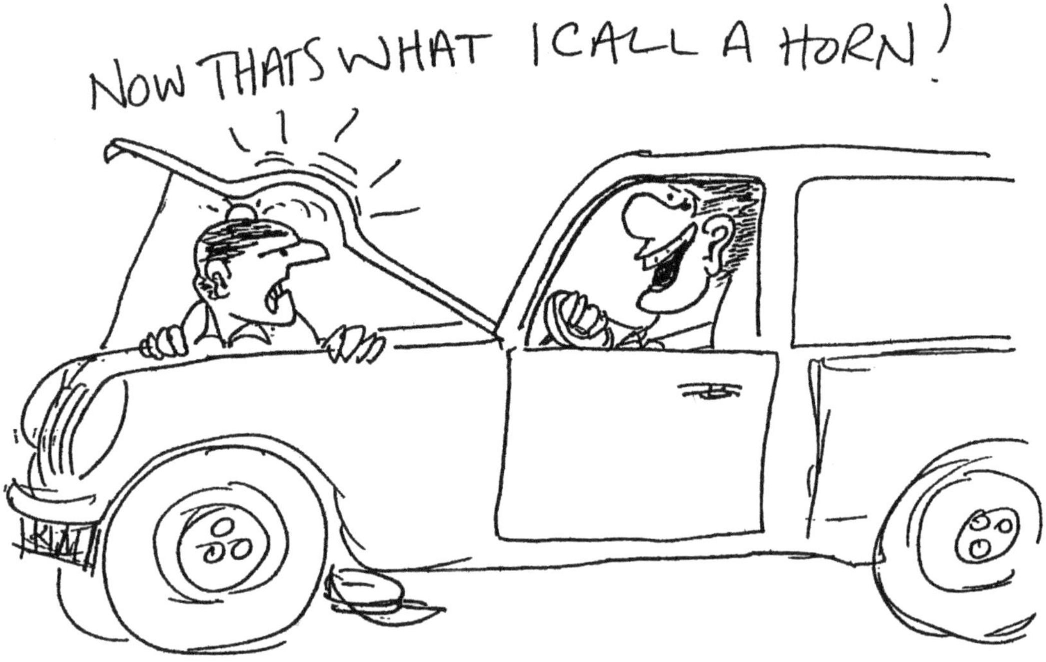
NOW THATS WHAT I CALL A HORN!

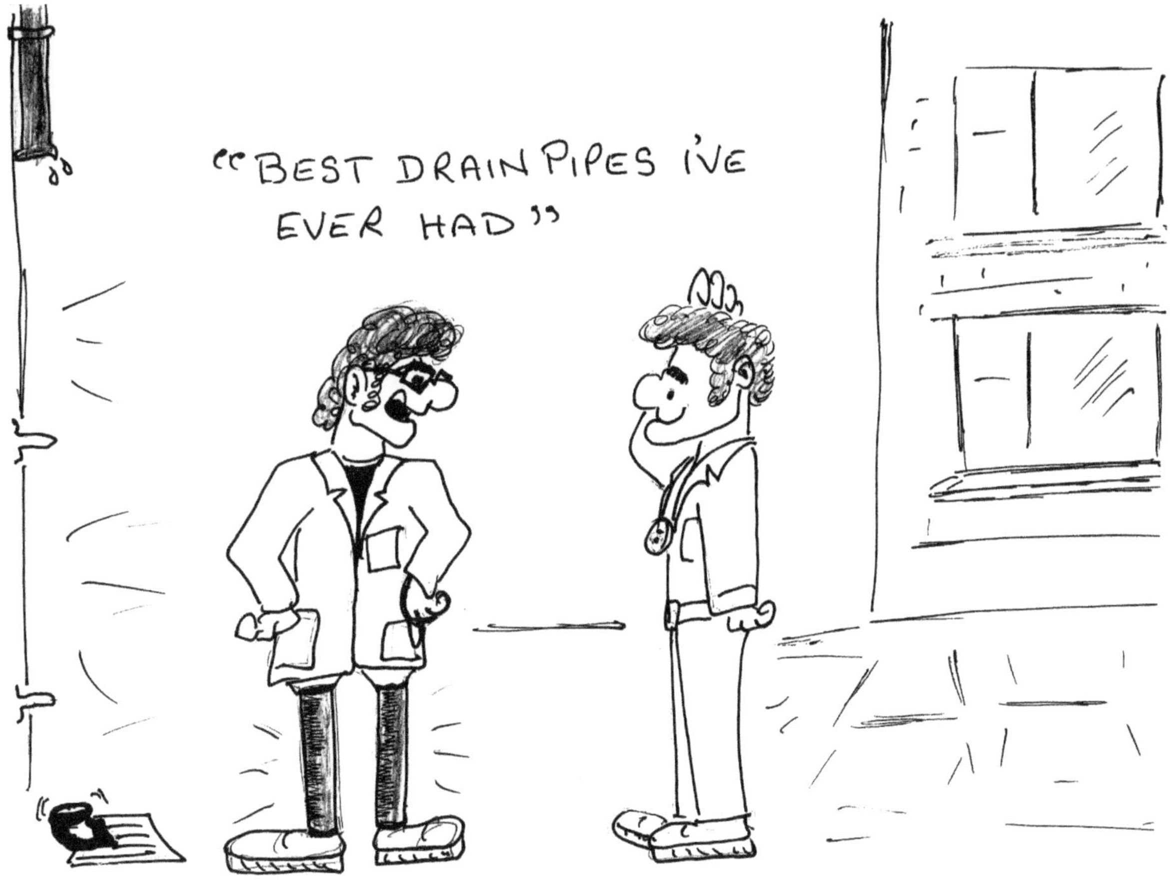
"BEST DRAIN PIPES I'VE EVER HAD"

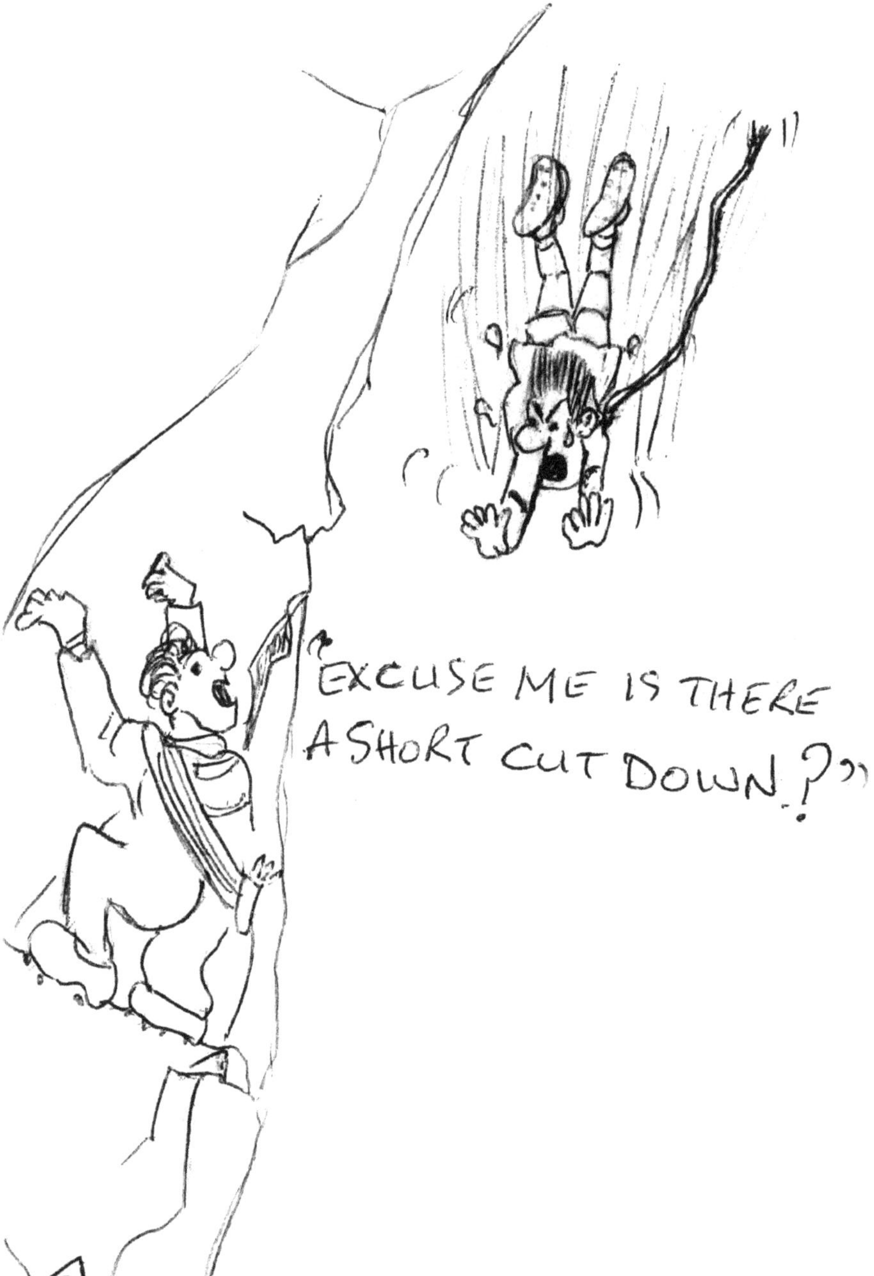
"EXCUSE ME IS THERE A SHORT CUT DOWN?!"

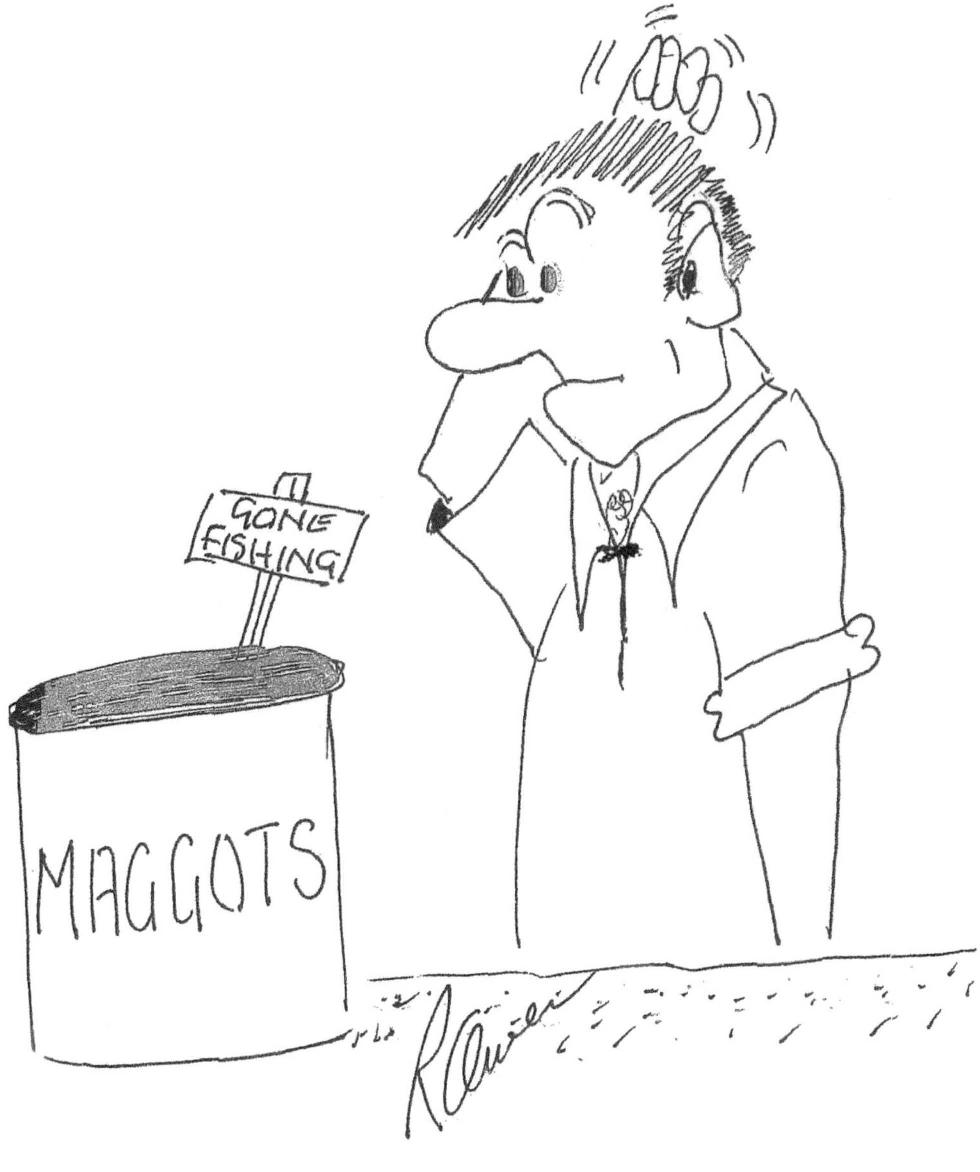
GONE FISHING
MAGGOTS

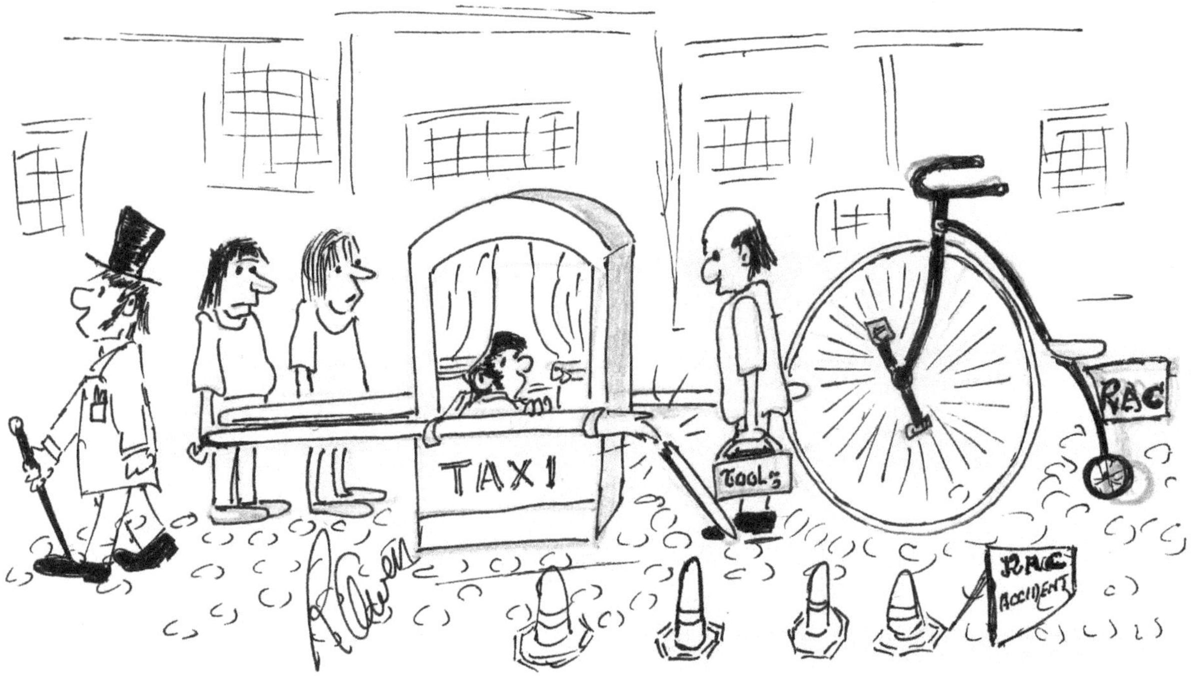
TAXI
TOOLS
RAC
RAC
ACCIDENT

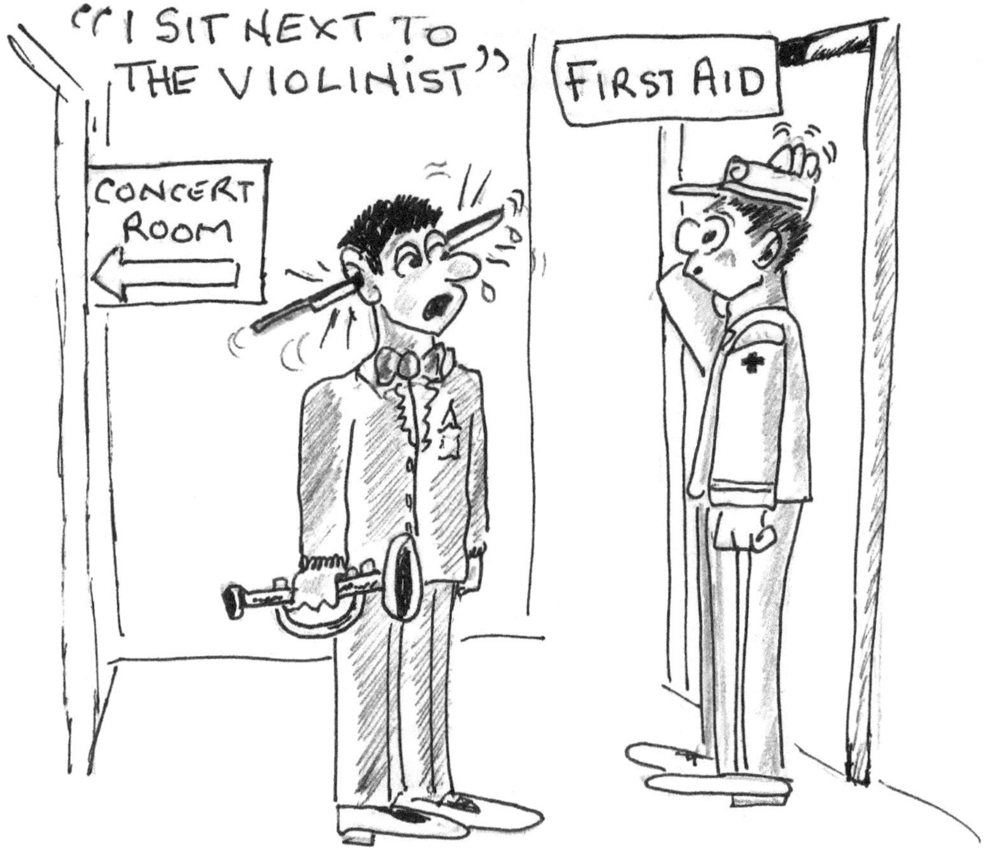
"I SIT NEXT TO THE VIOLINIST"
CONCERT ROOM
FIRST AID

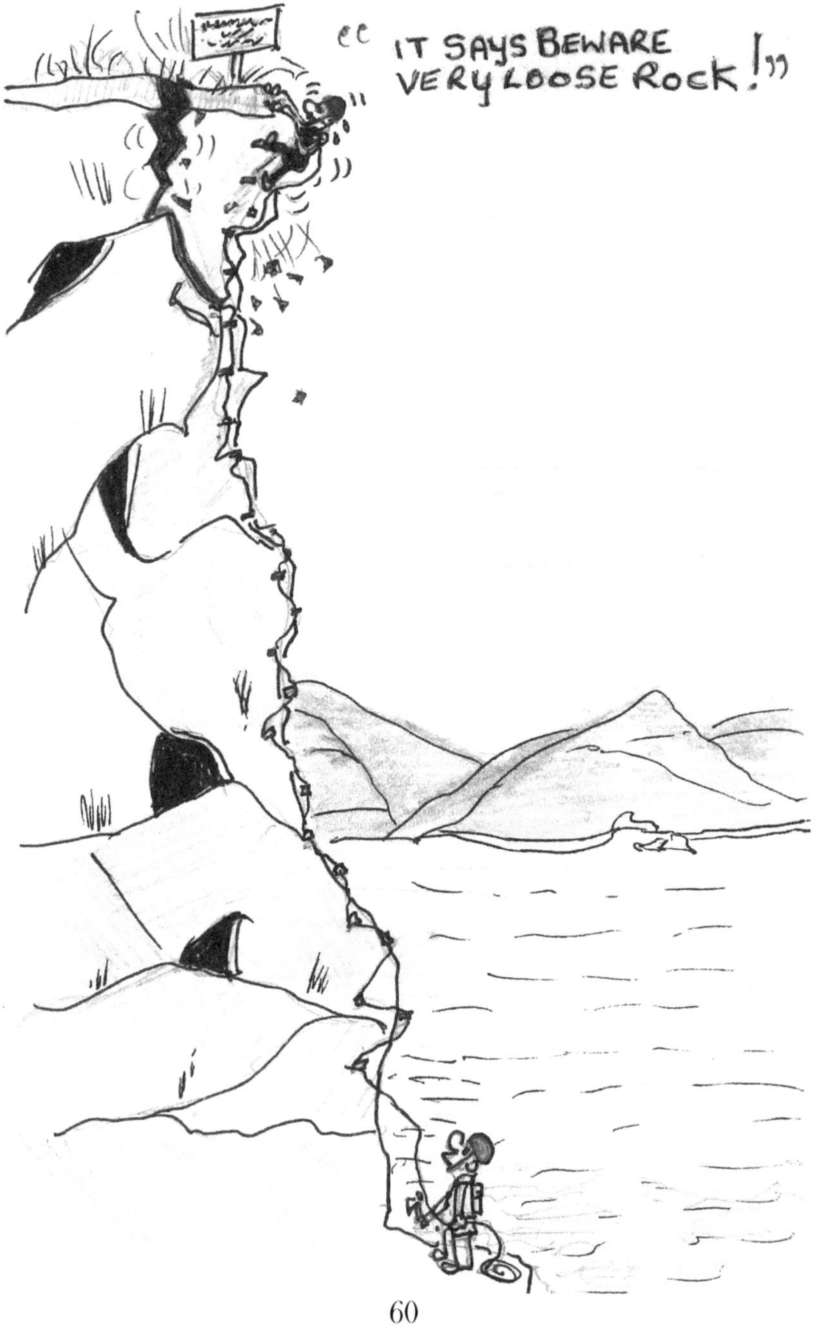
"IT SAYS BEWARE VERY LOOSE ROCK!"

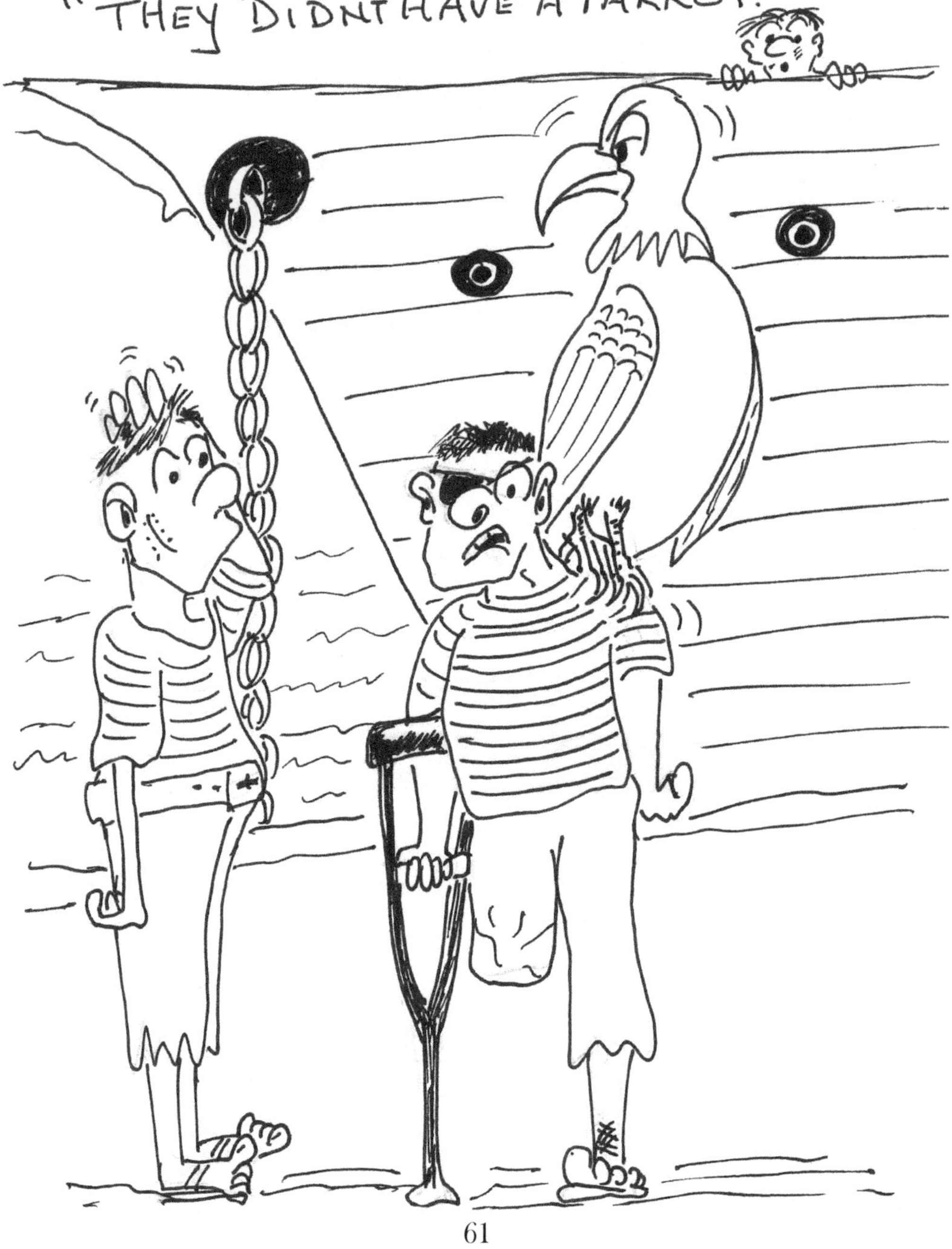

"THEY DIDN'T HAVE A PARROT."

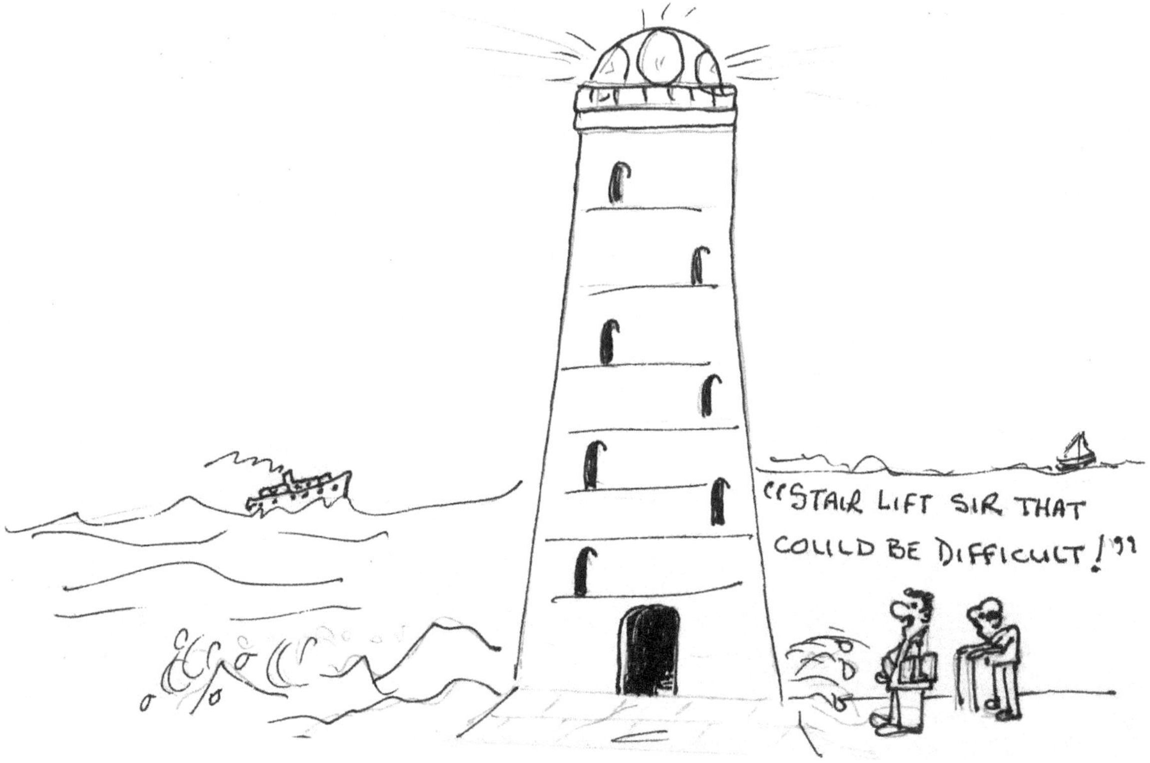
"STAIR LIFT SIR THAT COULD BE DIFFICULT!"

"FORGET YOUR NAVY DAYS YOU FOOL AND GET DOWN!"

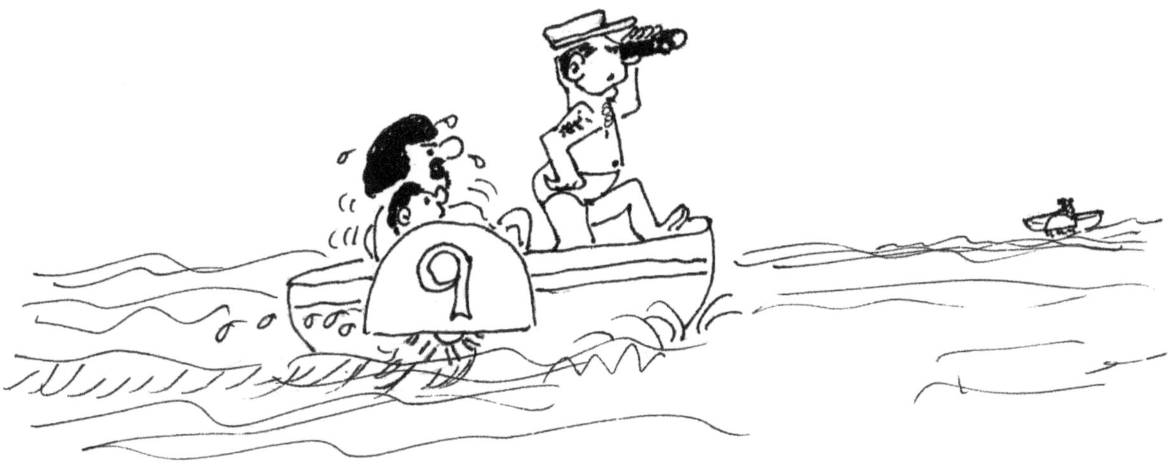

"I DONT KNOW ABOUT YOU BUT I FEEL
A LITTLE SLUGGISH TODAY!"

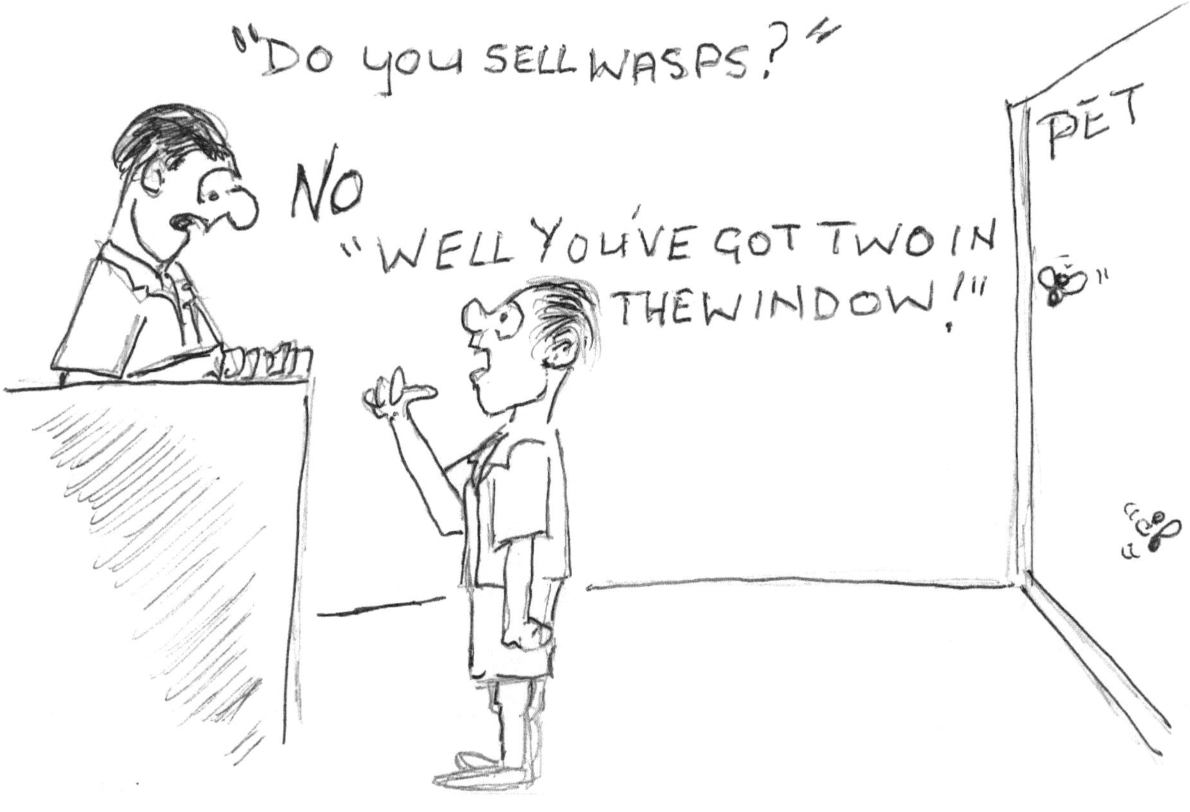
"DO YOU SELL WASPS?"
NO
"WELL YOU'VE GOT TWO IN THE WINDOW!"
PET

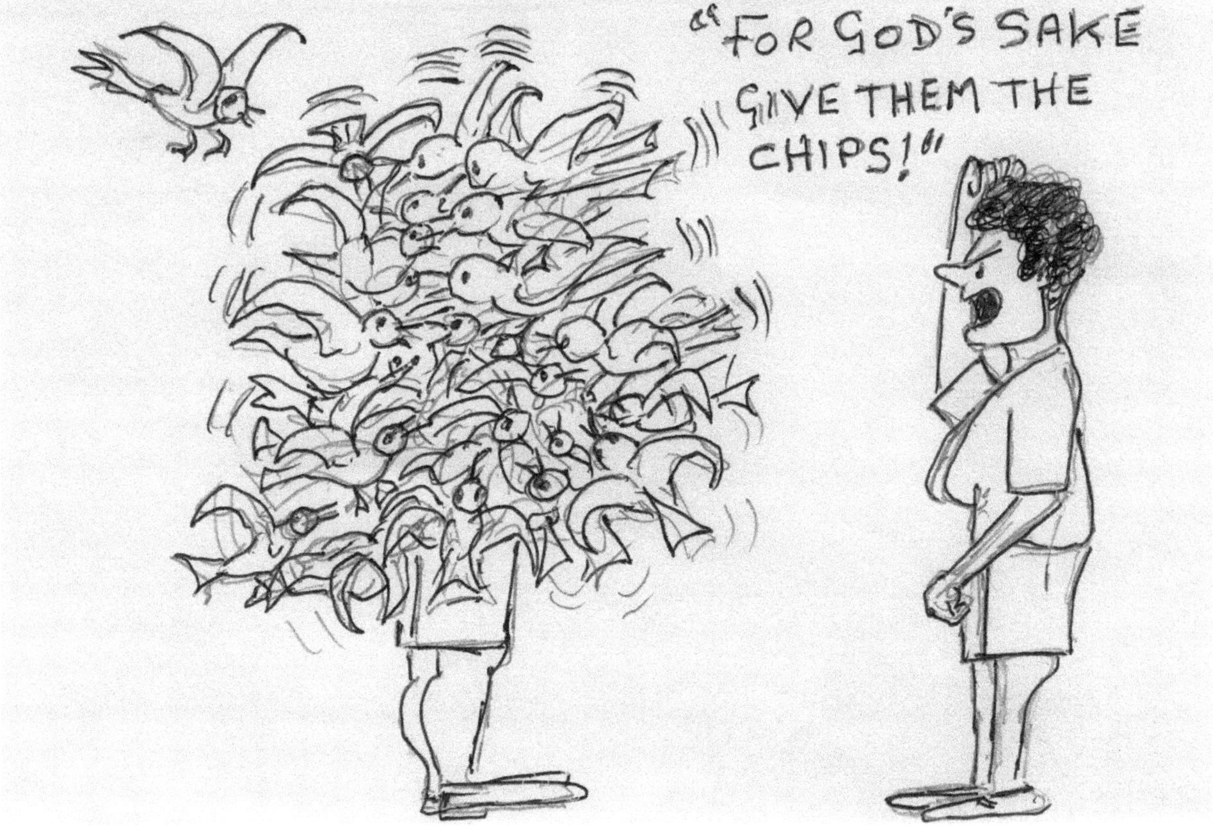
"FOR GOD'S SAKE
GIVE THEM THE
CHIPS!"

"I HATE COLD WATER"

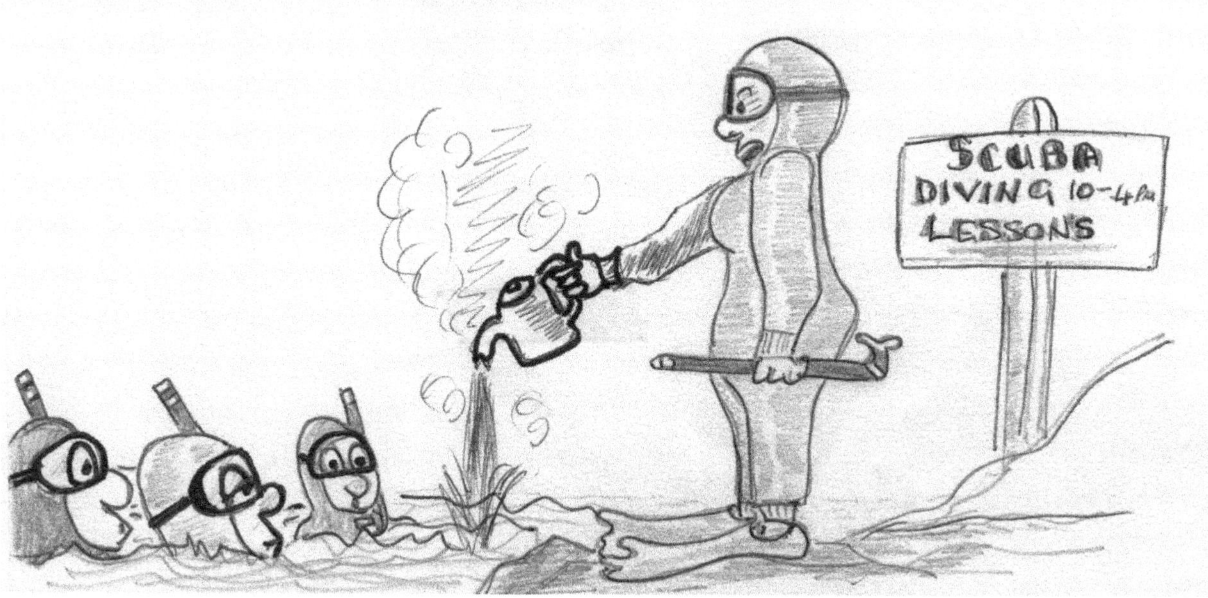
SCUBA
DIVING 10-4PM
LESSONS

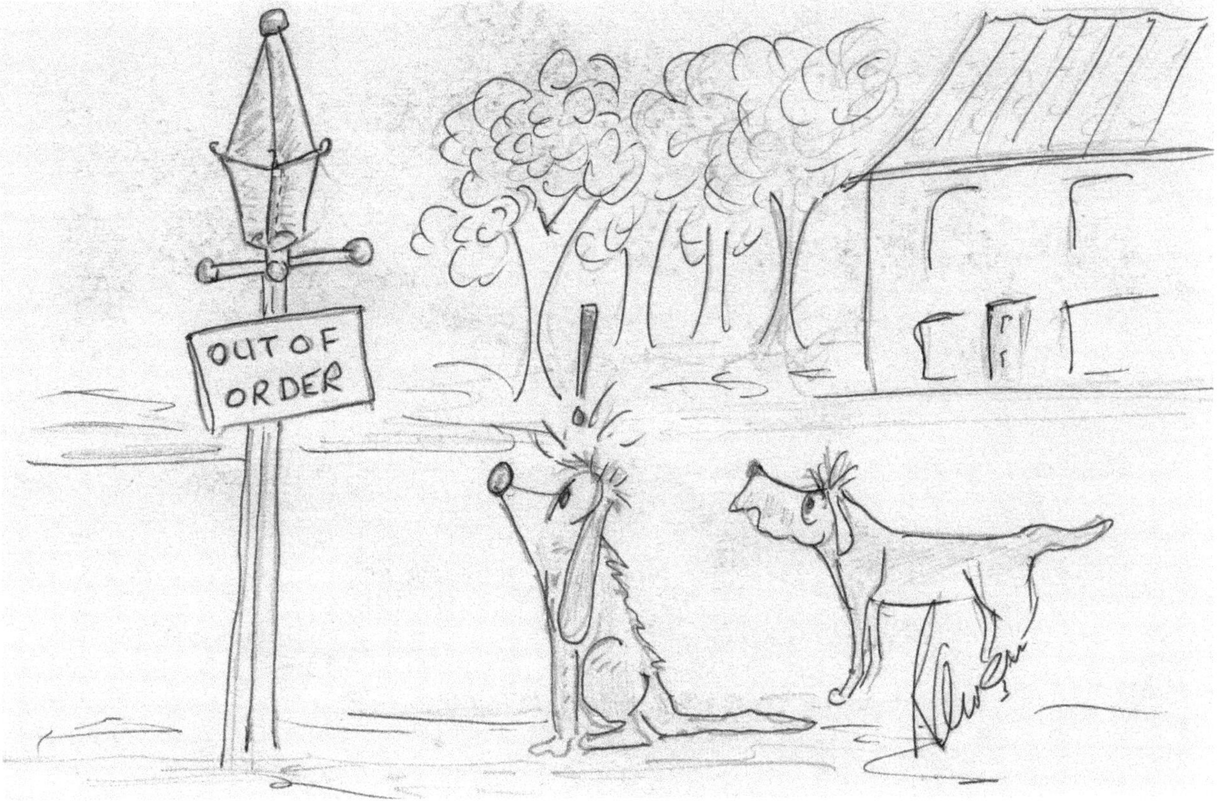
OUT OF
ORDER

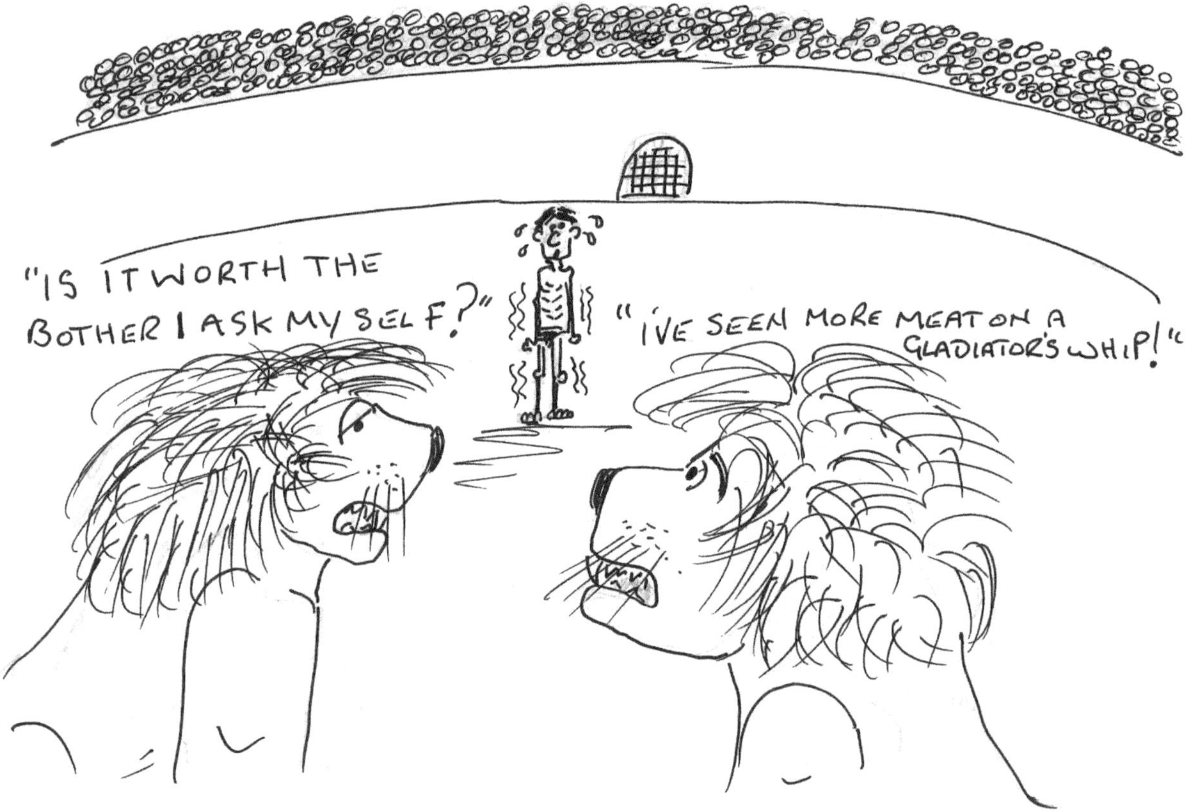
"IS IT WORTH THE BOTHER I ASK MY SELF?"
"I'VE SEEN MORE MEAT ON A GLADIATOR'S WHIP!"

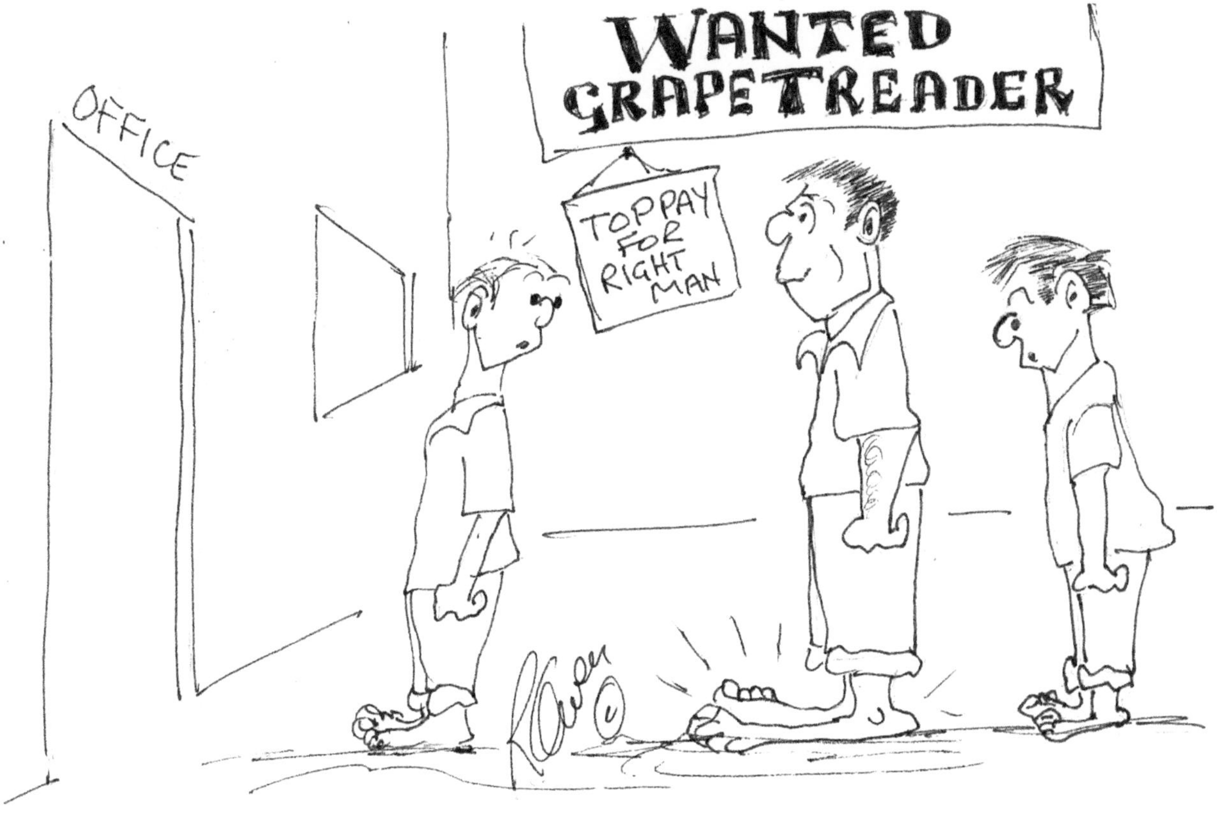

OFFICE
WANTED
GRAPE TREADER
TOP PAY FOR RIGHT MAN

"LOOKS LIKE HARRY'S GOT ANOTHER BAD LOSER!"

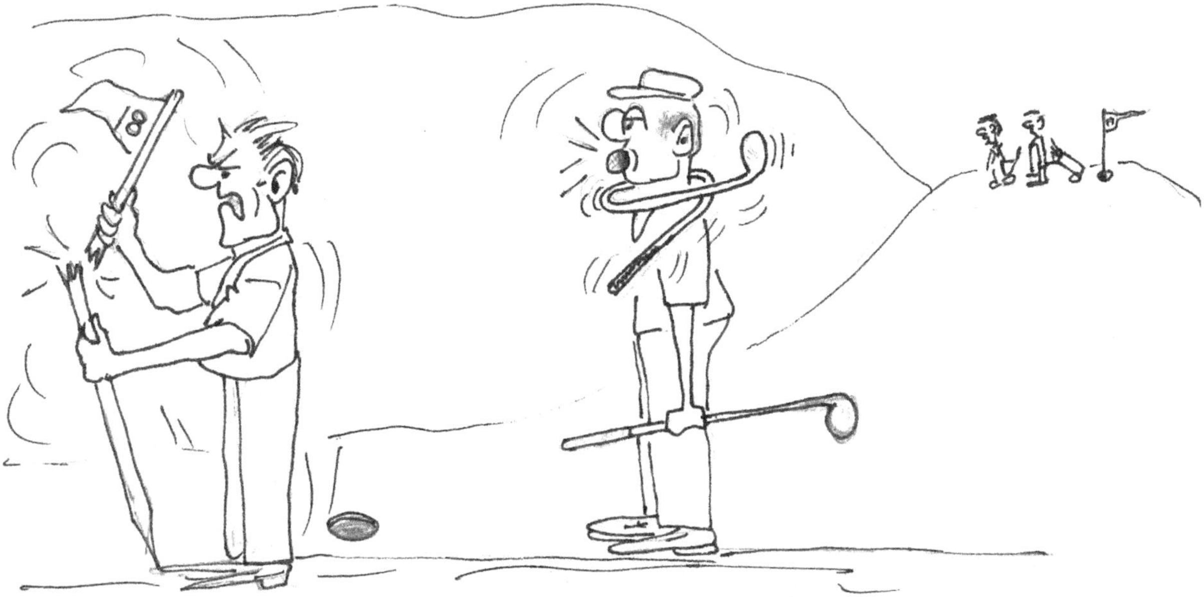

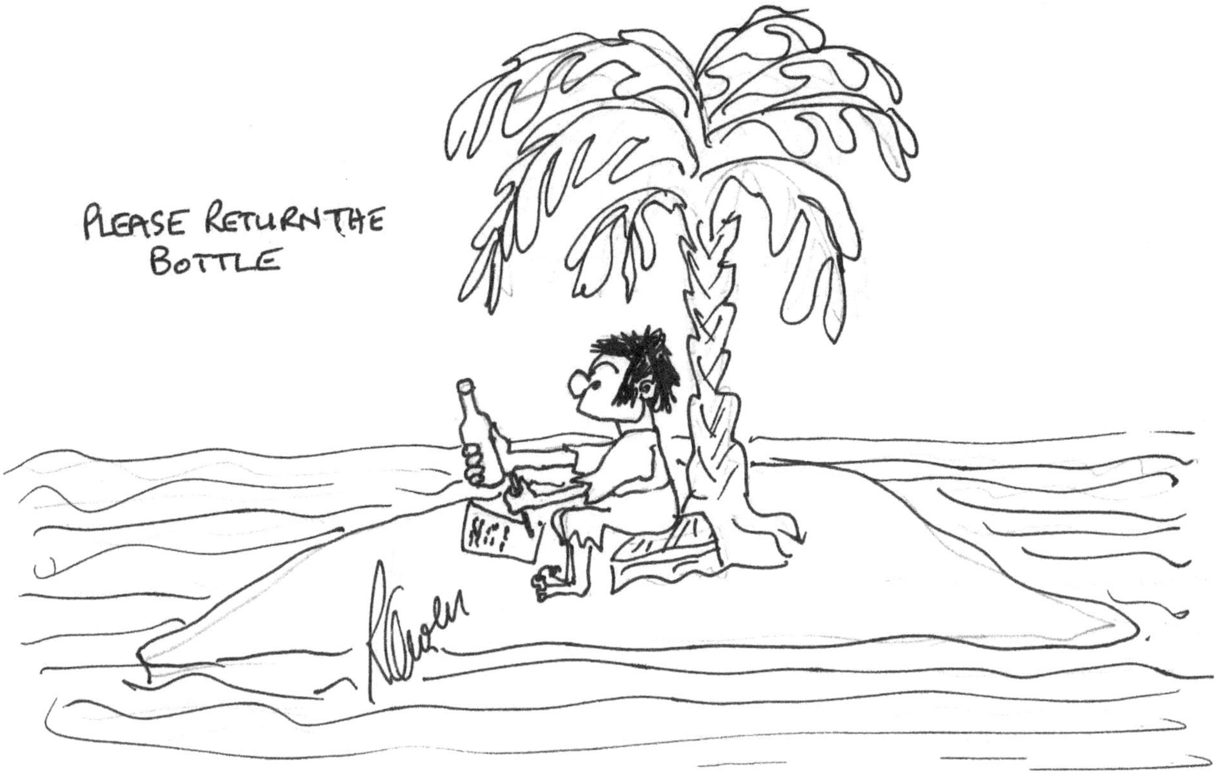
PLEASE RETURN THE BOTTLE

"LET'S PUT CANDLES ON HIS CAKE YOU SAID!"

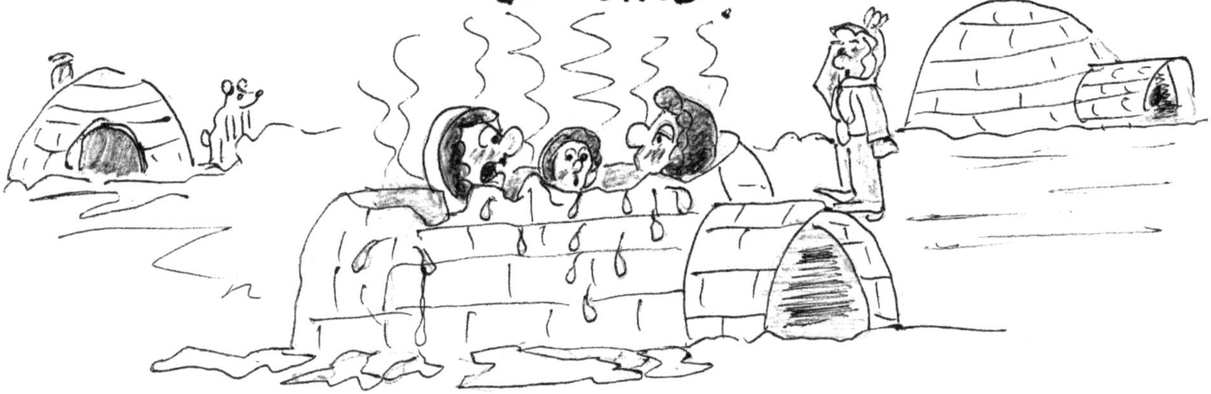

"DID YOU REMEMBER THE CAN OPENER LUV!"

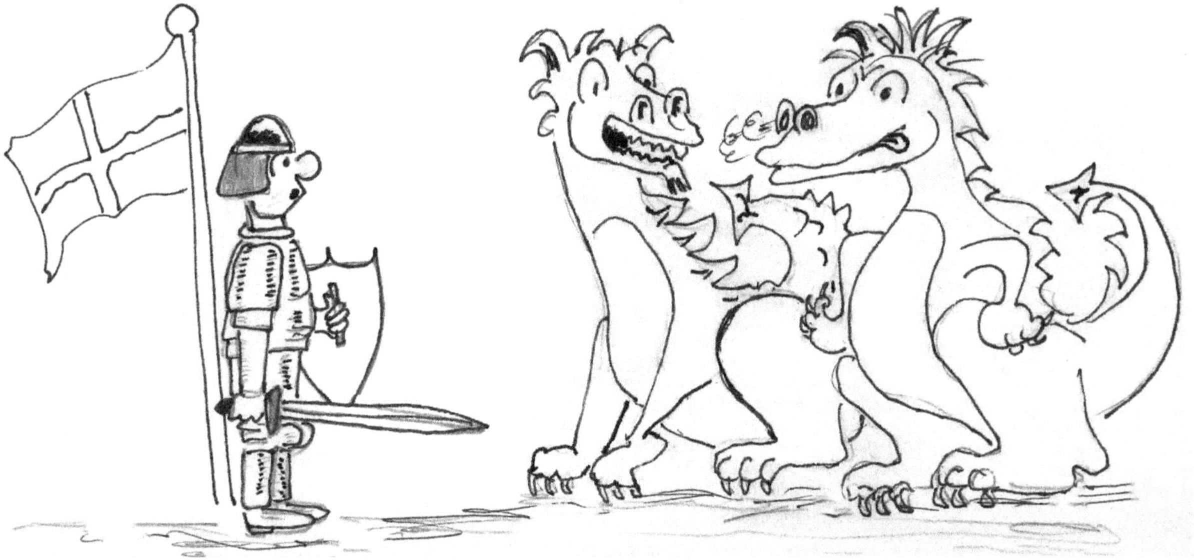

"LOOK PADDY WE'RE SAVED
HERE COMES THE **TITANIC**!"

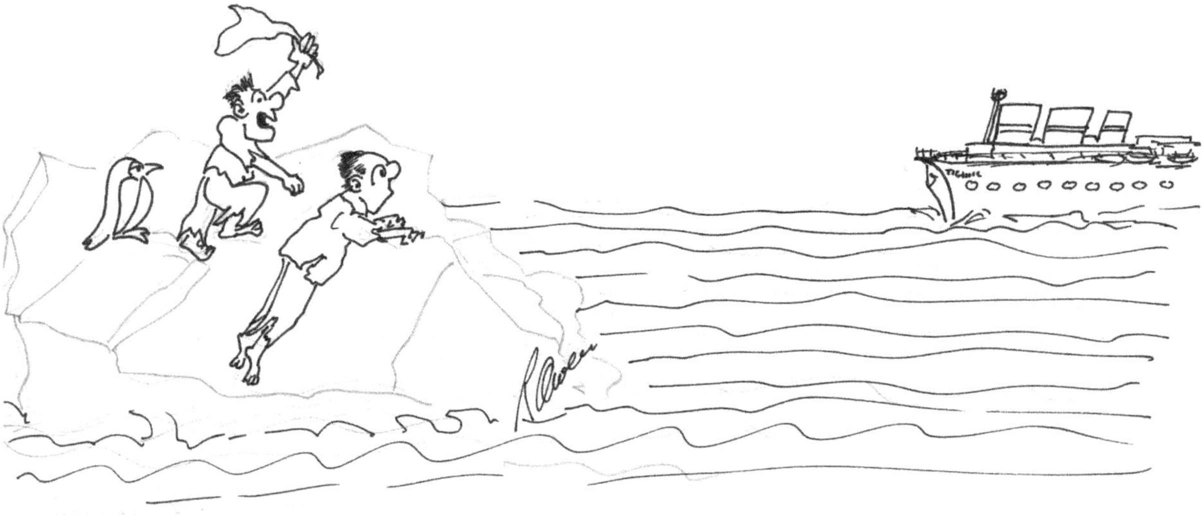

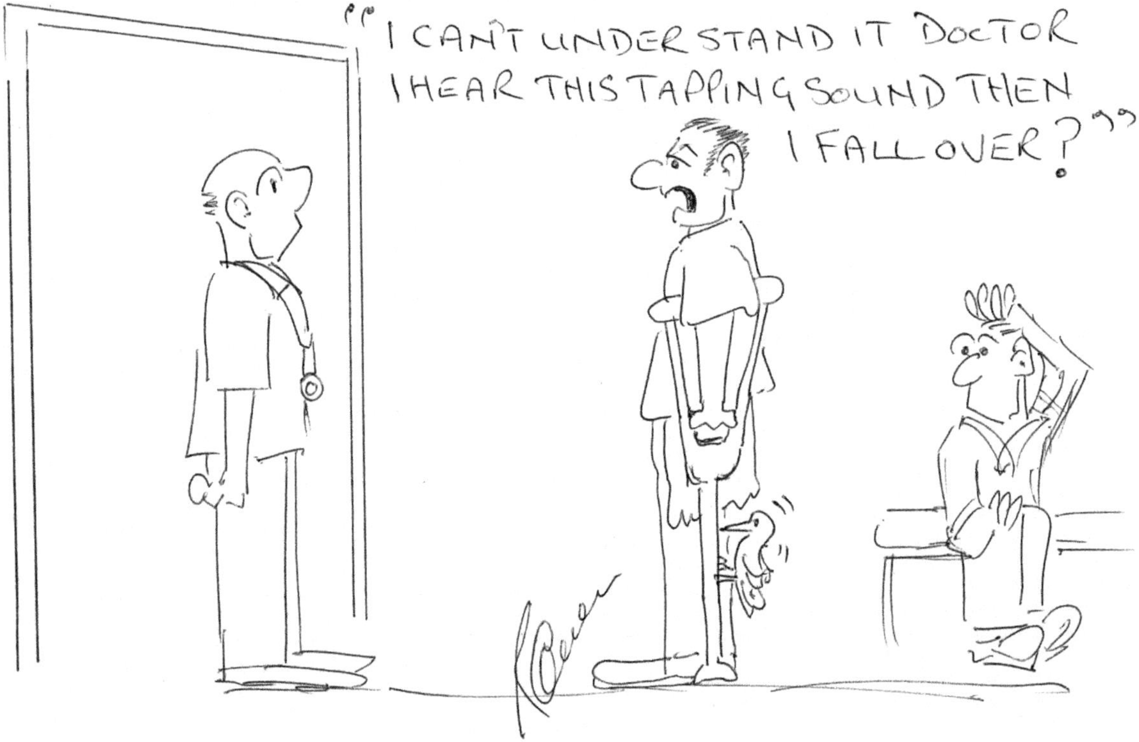
"I CAN'T UNDERSTAND IT DOCTOR
I HEAR THIS TAPPING SOUND THEN
I FALL OVER?"

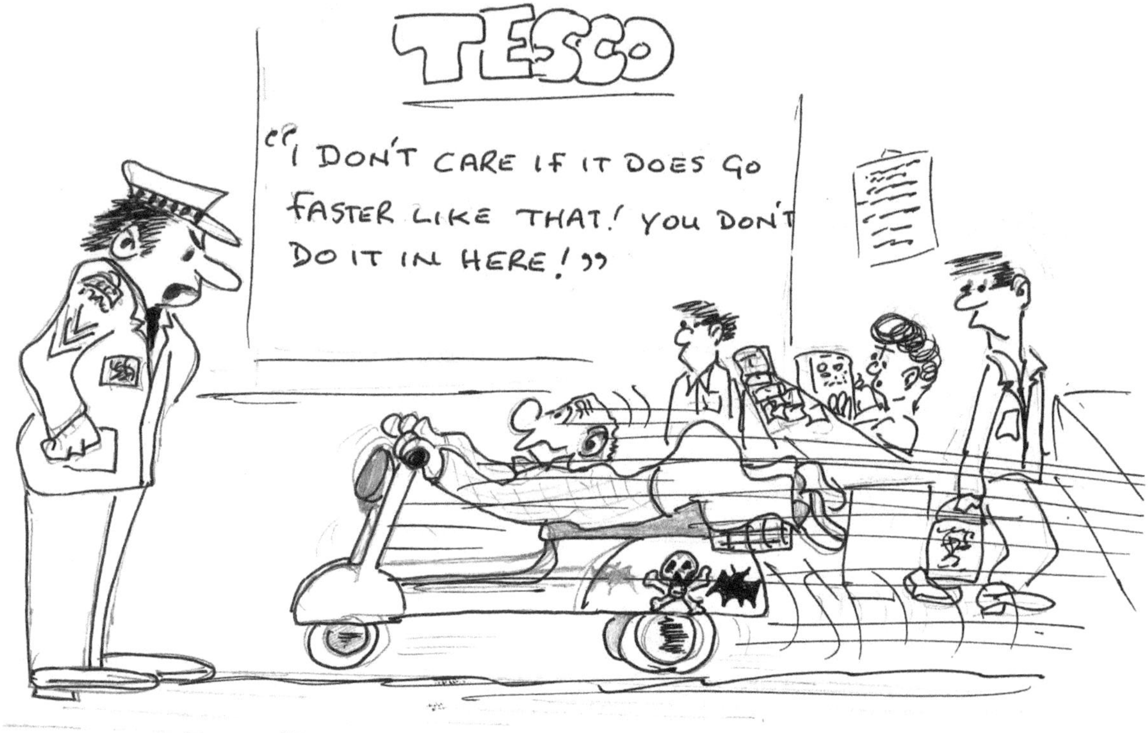
TESCO
"I DON'T CARE IF IT DOES GO FASTER LIKE THAT! YOU DON'T DO IT IN HERE!"

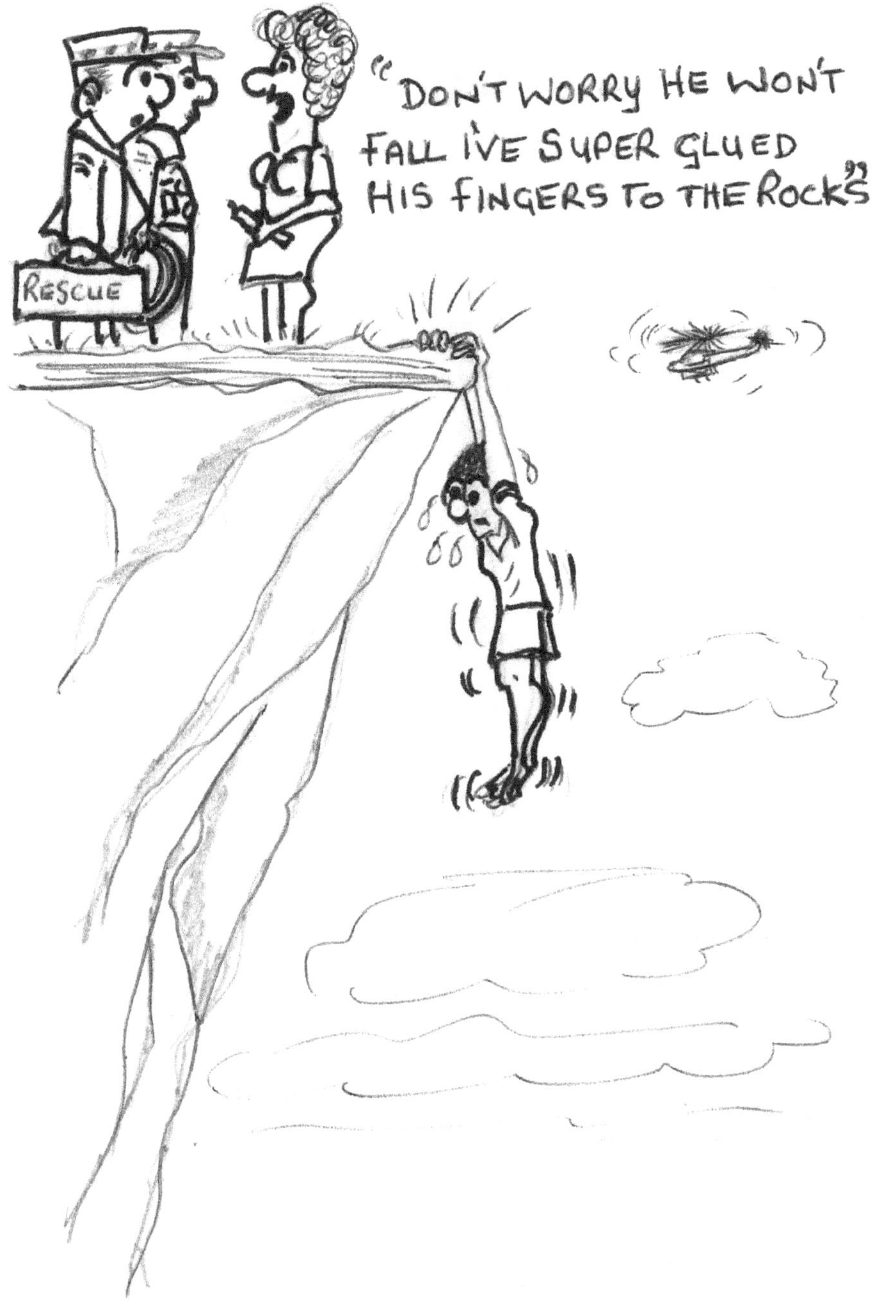
"DON'T WORRY HE WON'T FALL I'VE SUPER GLUED HIS FINGERS TO THE ROCKS"
RESCUE

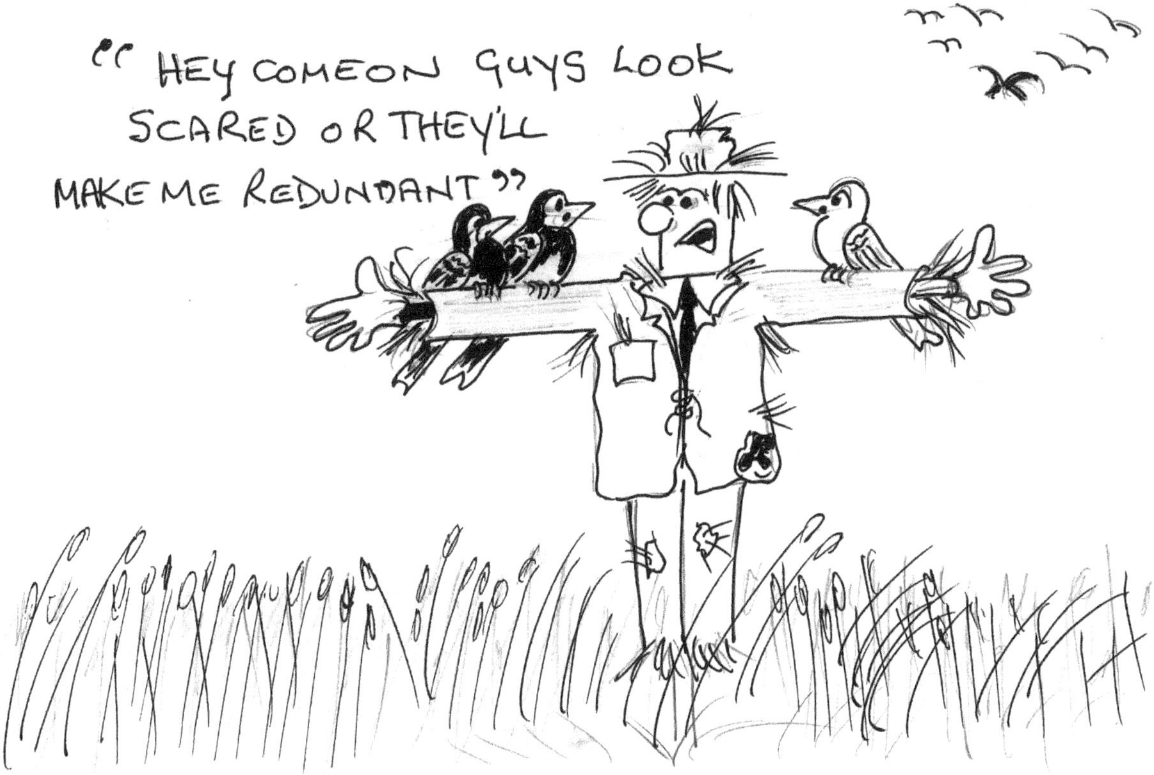
"HEY COMEON GUYS LOOK SCARED OR THEY'LL MAKE ME REDUNDANT"

"IT SAYS WORLD CHAMPION HIDE AND SEEK 1951"

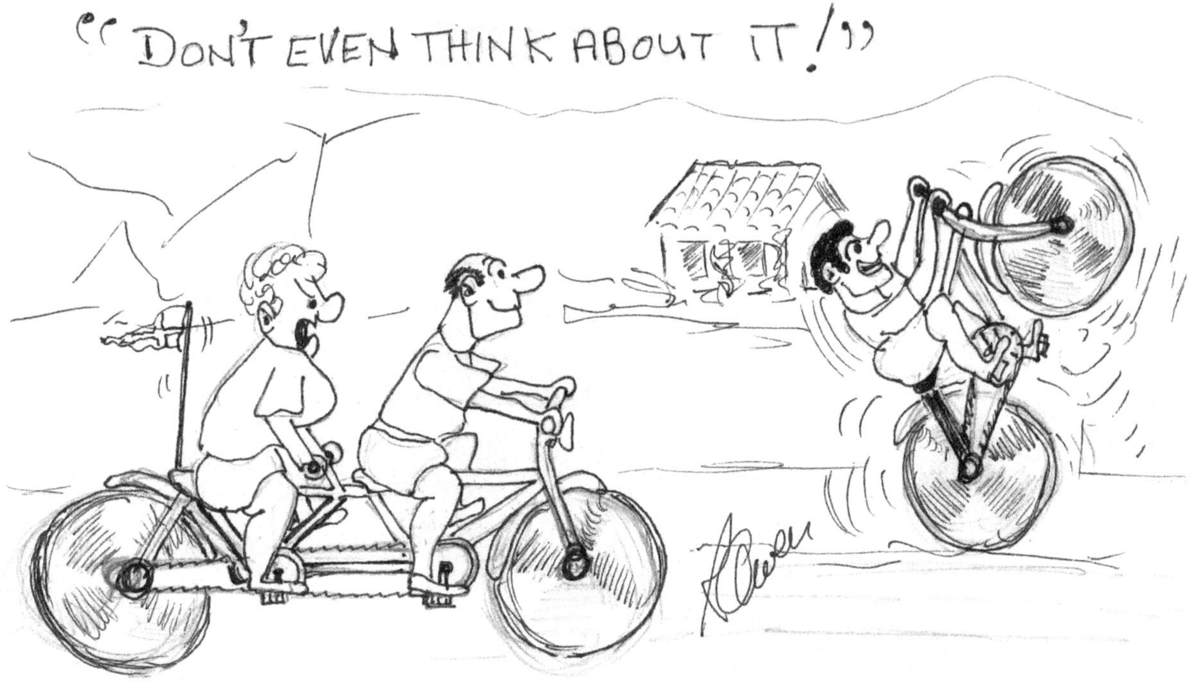
"DON'T EVEN THINK ABOUT IT!"

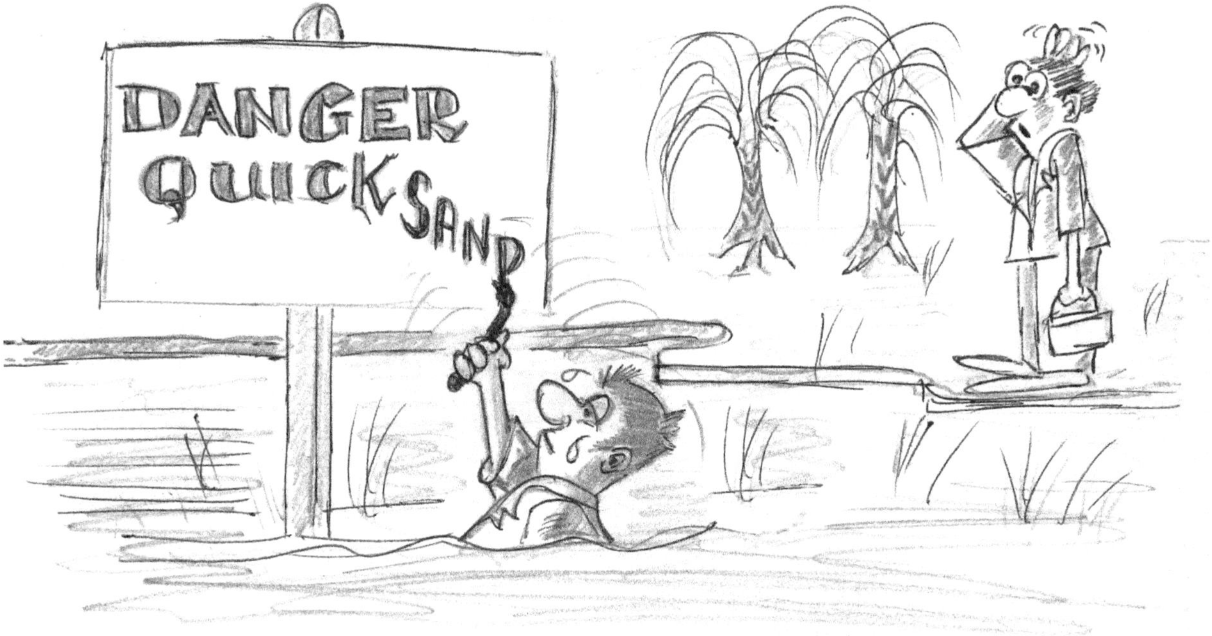
DANGER
QUICKSAND

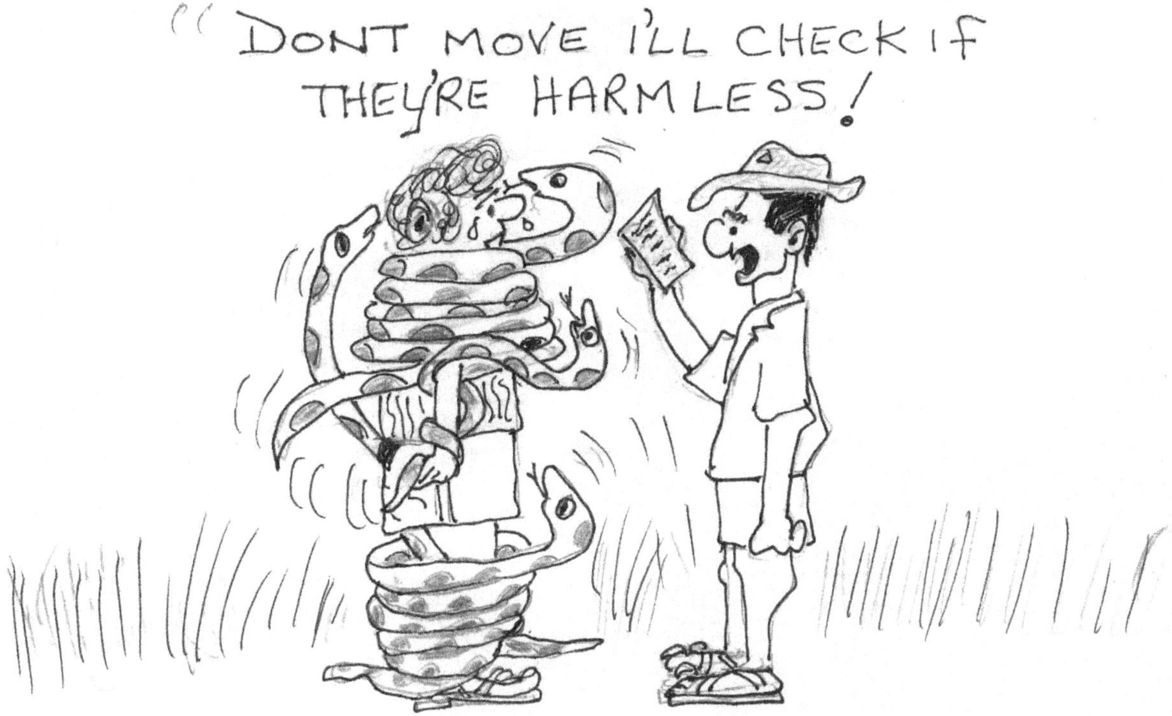
"DONT MOVE I'LL CHECK IF THEY'RE HARMLESS!

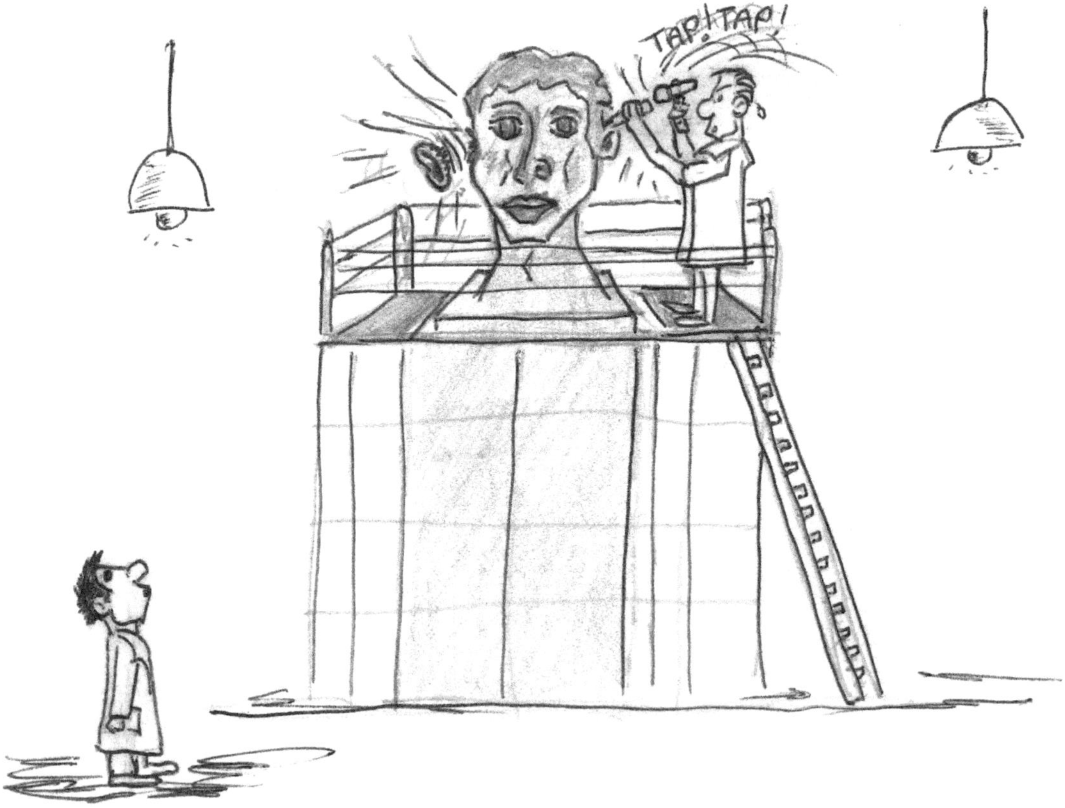
TAP! TAP!

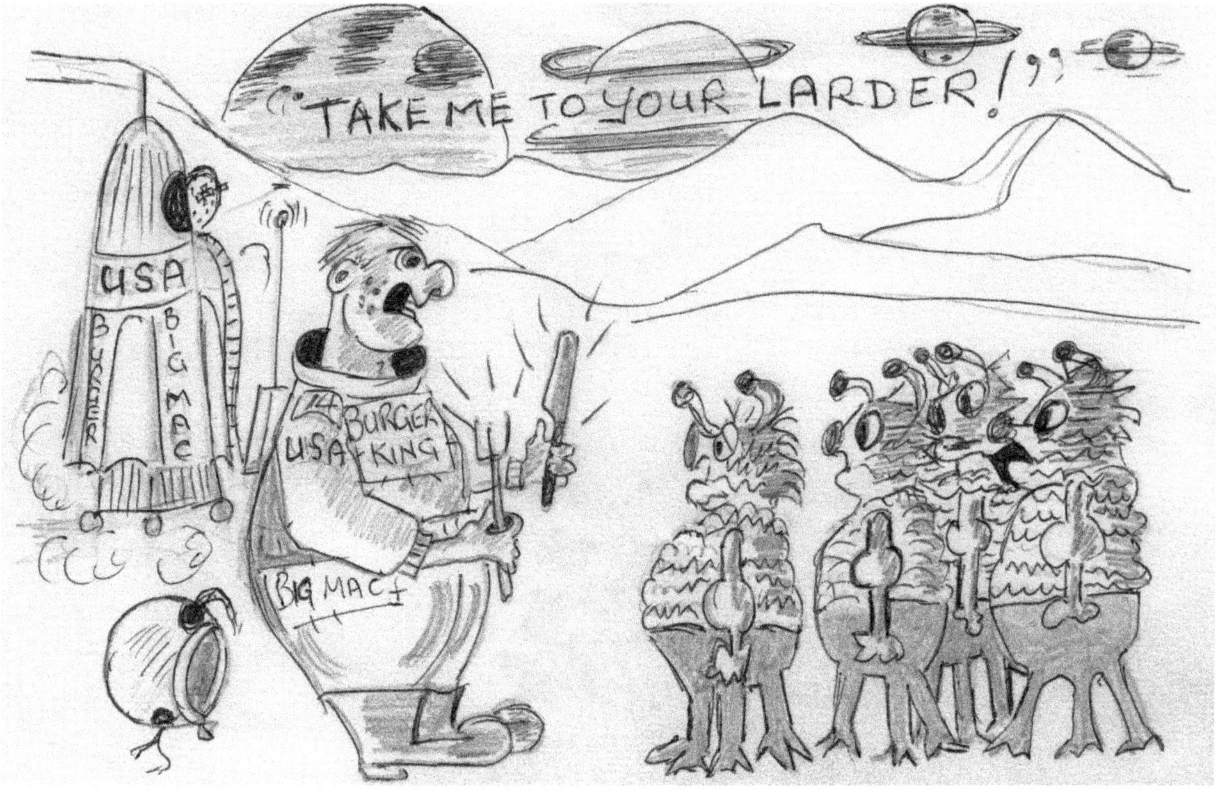
"TAKE ME TO YOUR LARDER!"
USA
BURGER
BIG MAC
USA
BURGER KING
BIG MAC

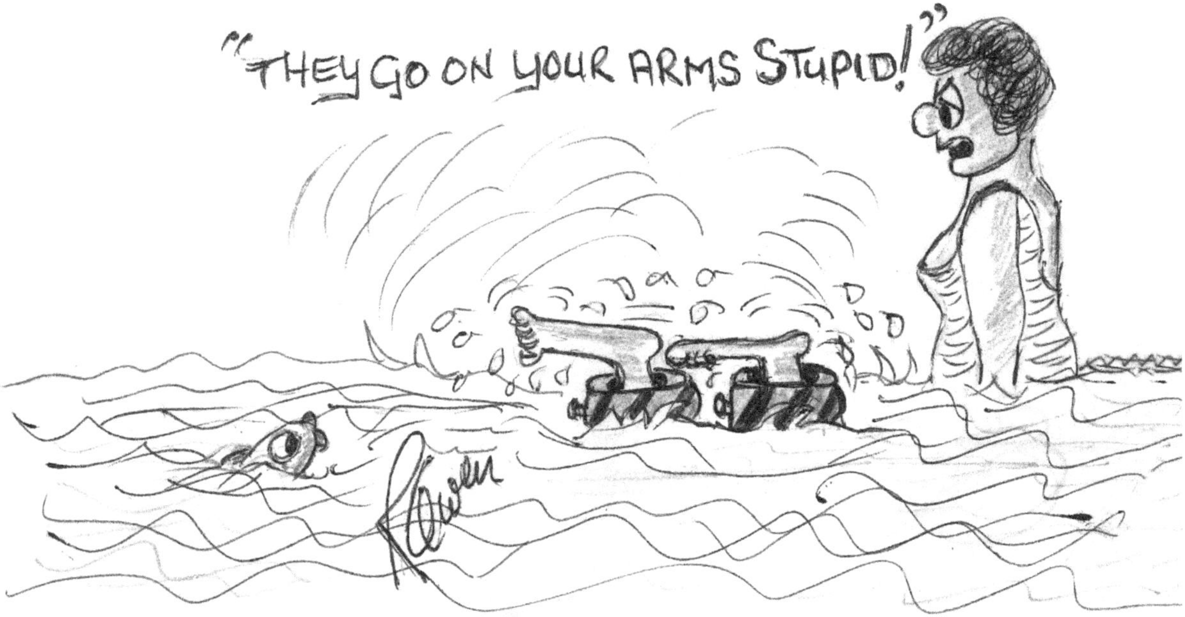
"THEY GO ON YOUR ARMS STUPID!"

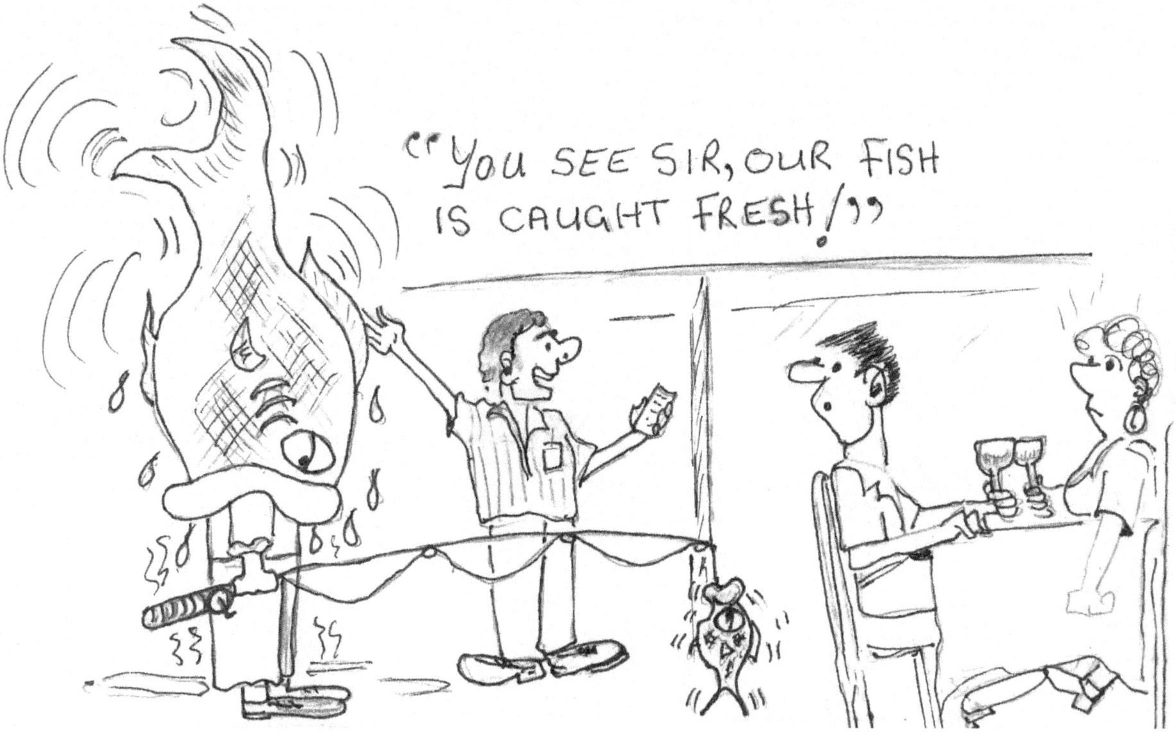
"YOU SEE SIR, OUR FISH
IS CAUGHT FRESH!"

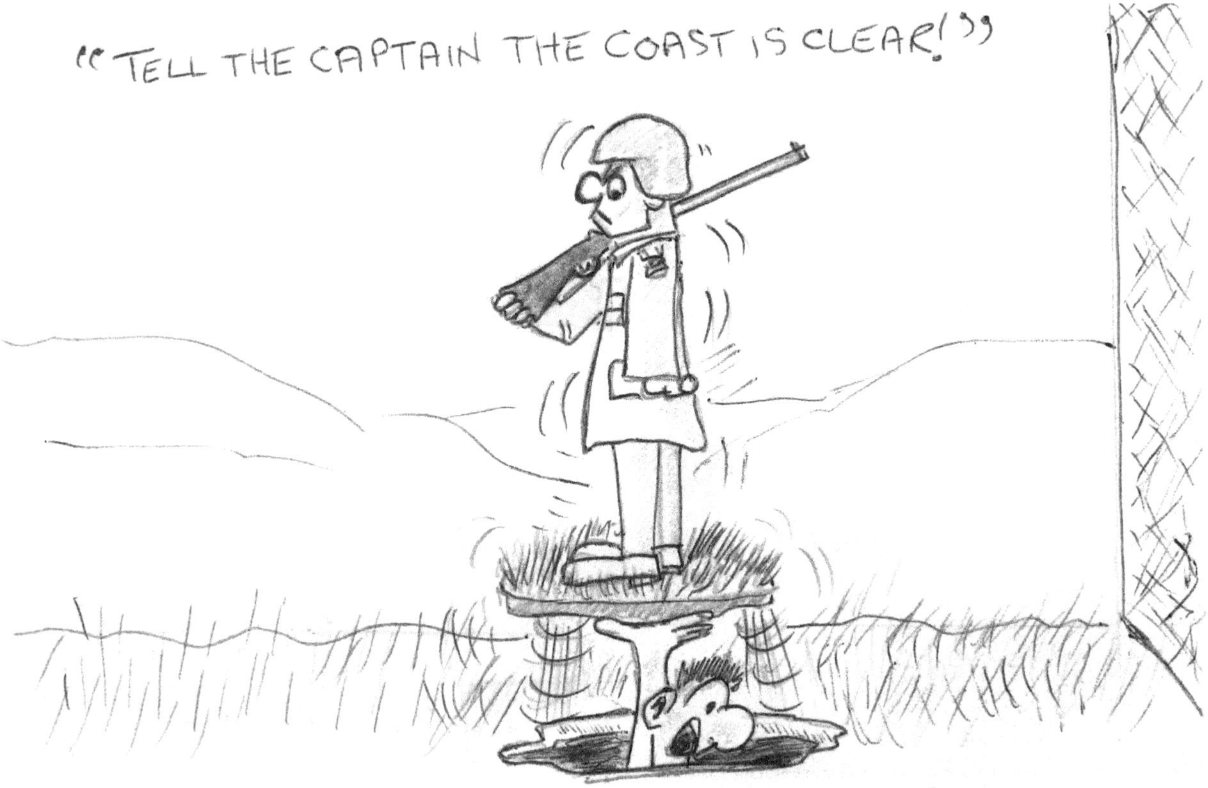
"TELL THE CAPTAIN THE COAST IS CLEAR!"

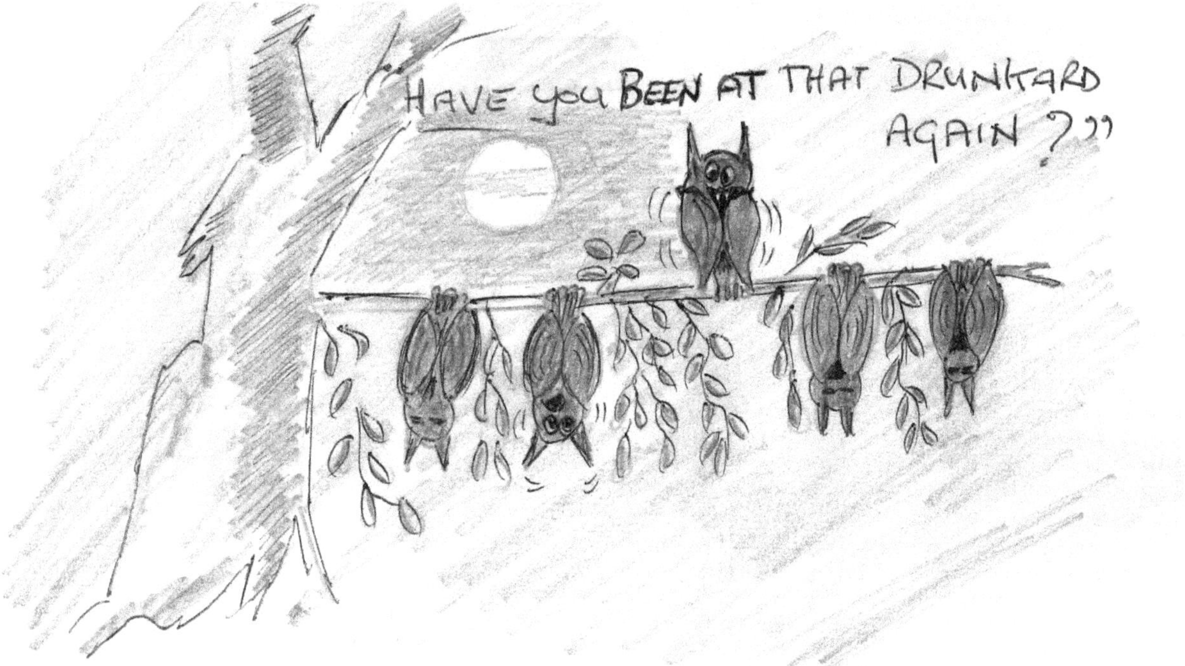
HAVE YOU BEEN AT THAT DRUNKARD AGAIN?"

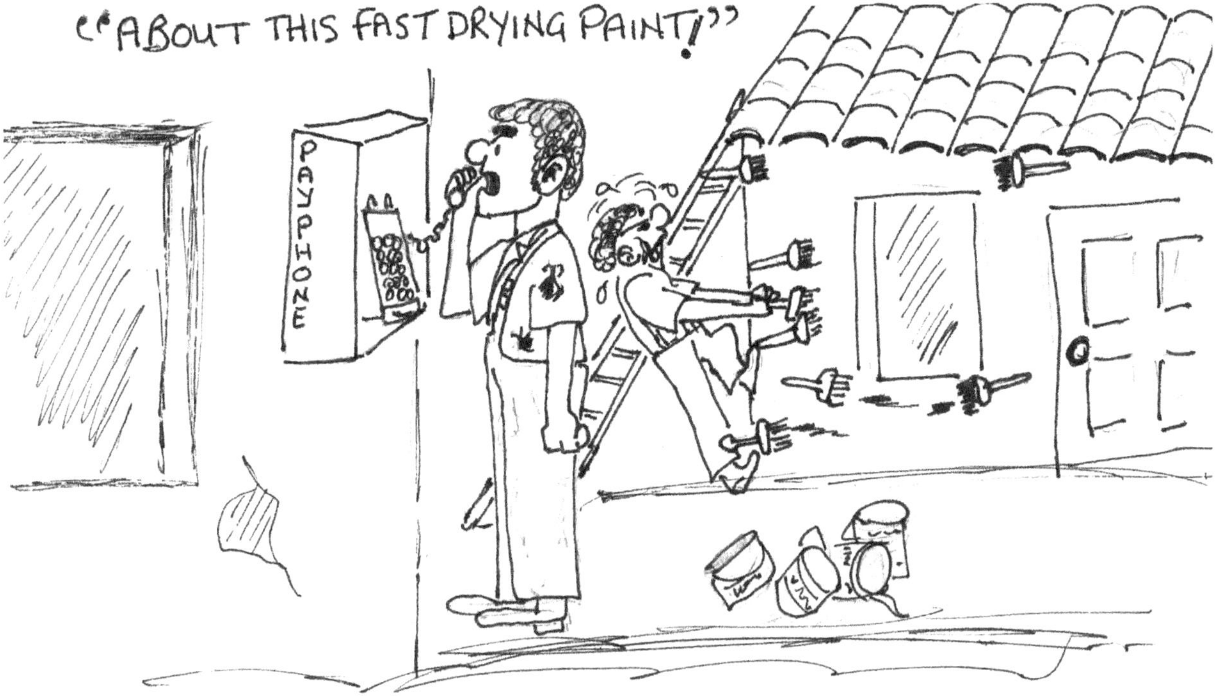
"ABOUT THIS FAST DRYING PAINT!"
PAYPHONE

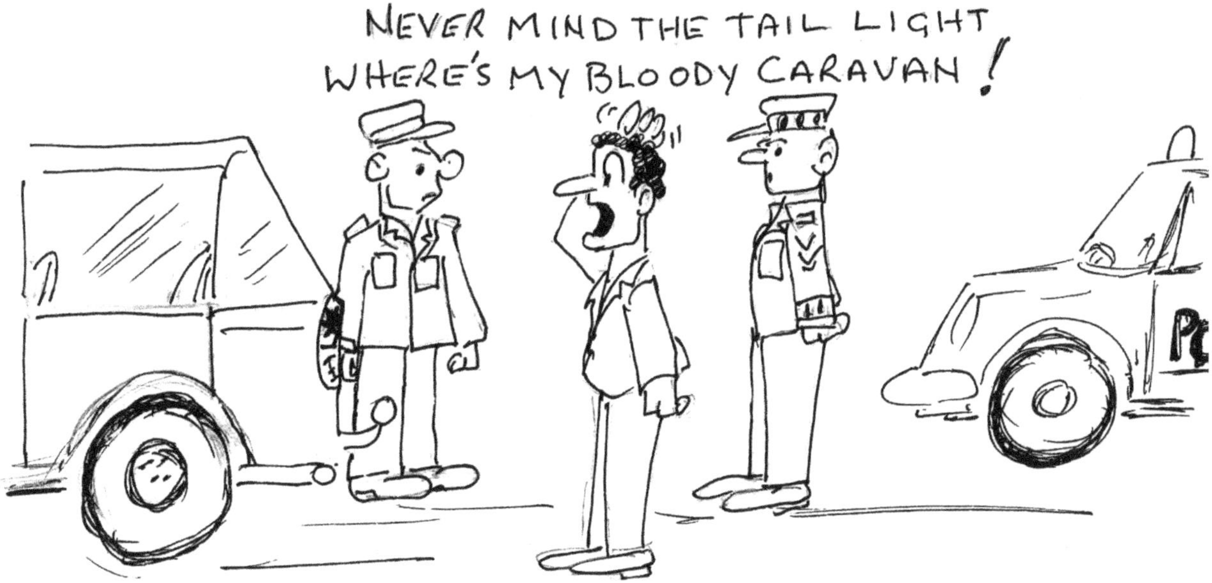
NEVER MIND THE TAIL LIGHT
WHERE'S MY BLOODY CARAVAN!

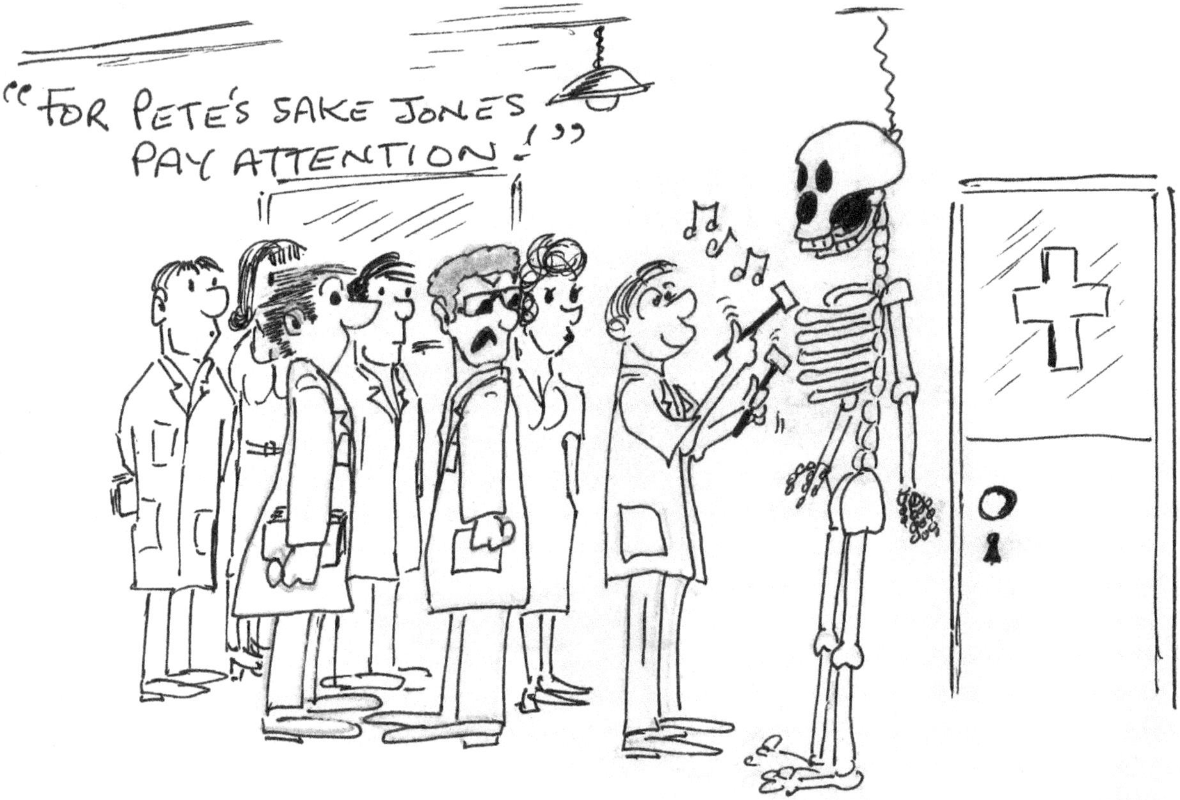
"FOR PETE'S SAKE JONES PAY ATTENTION!"

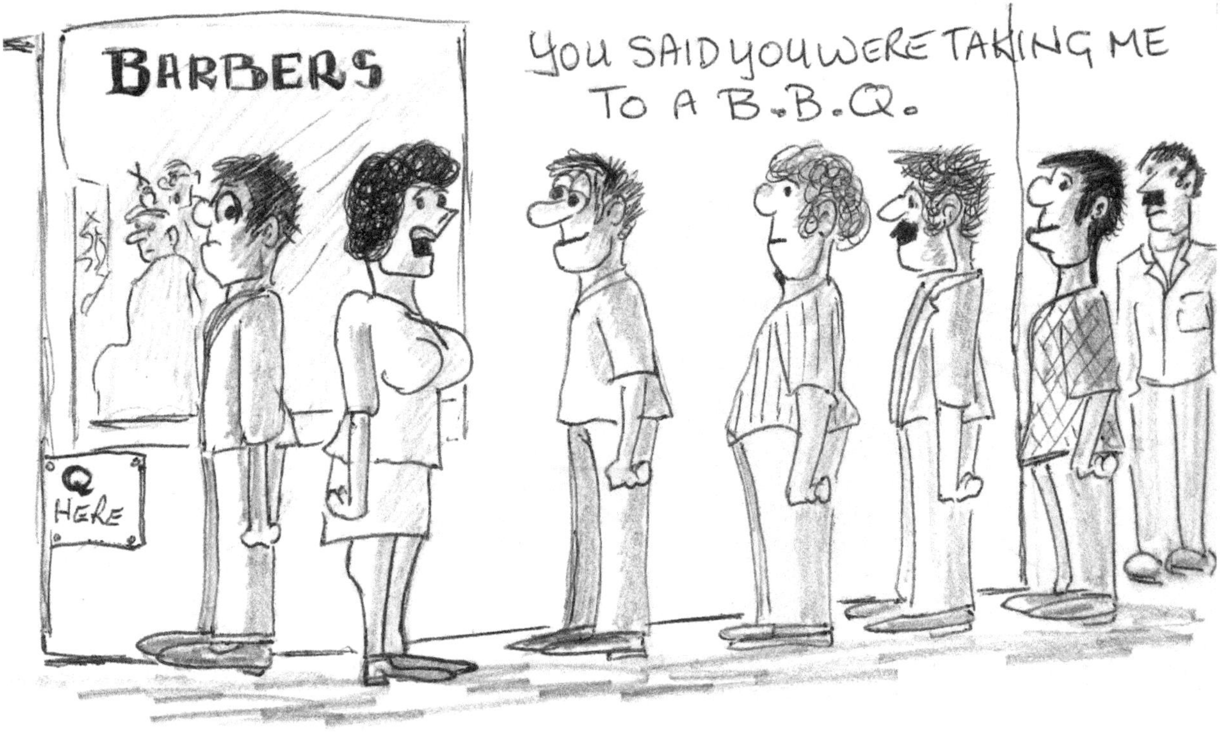
BARBERS
Q HERE
YOU SAID YOU WERE TAKING ME TO A B.B.Q.

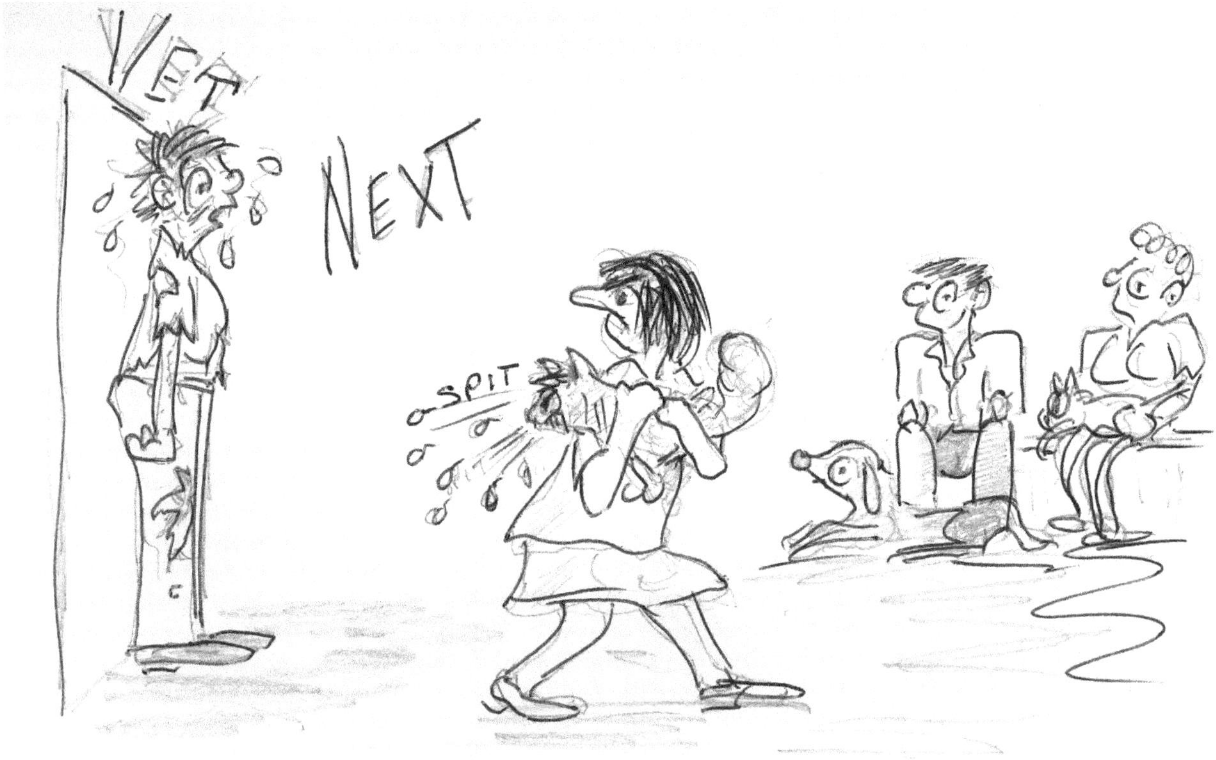
VET
NEXT
SPIT

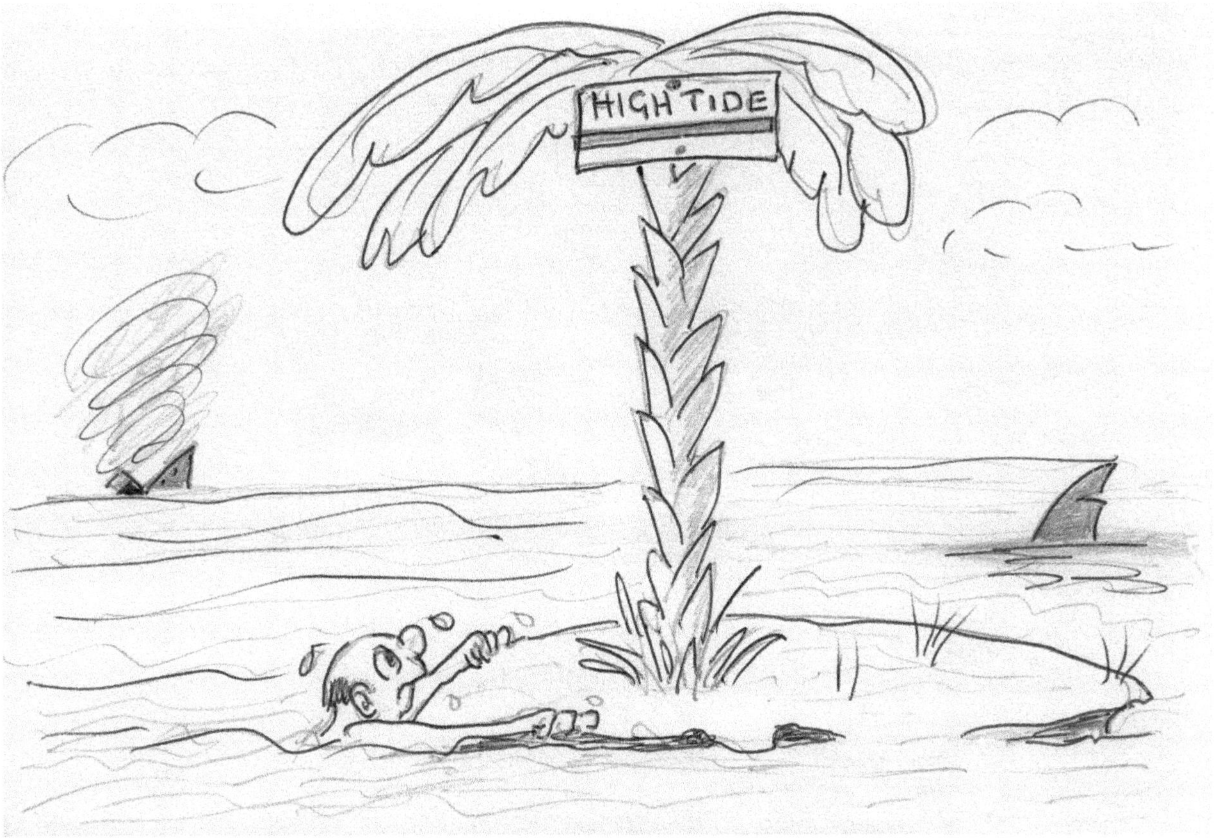
HIGH TIDE

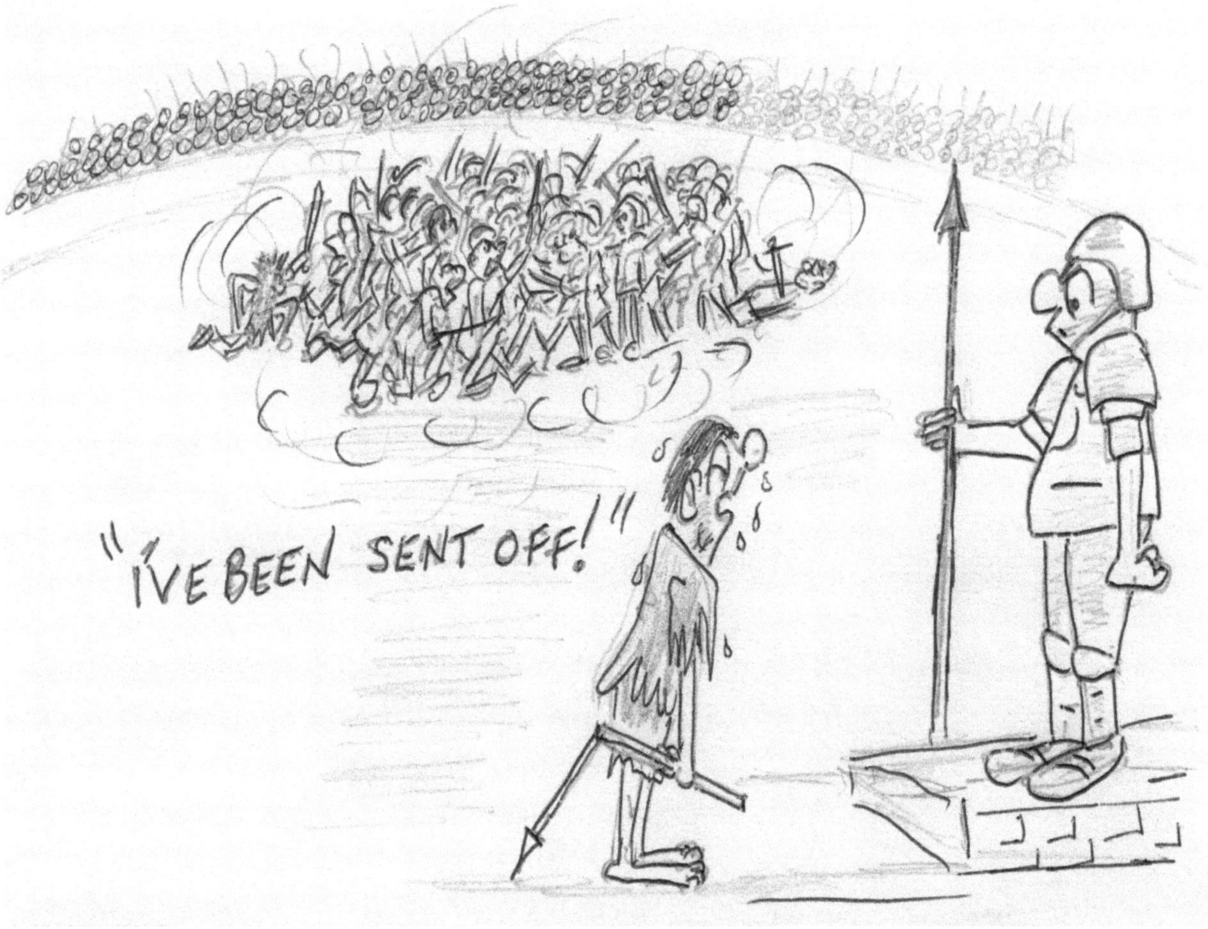
"I'VE BEEN SENT OFF!"

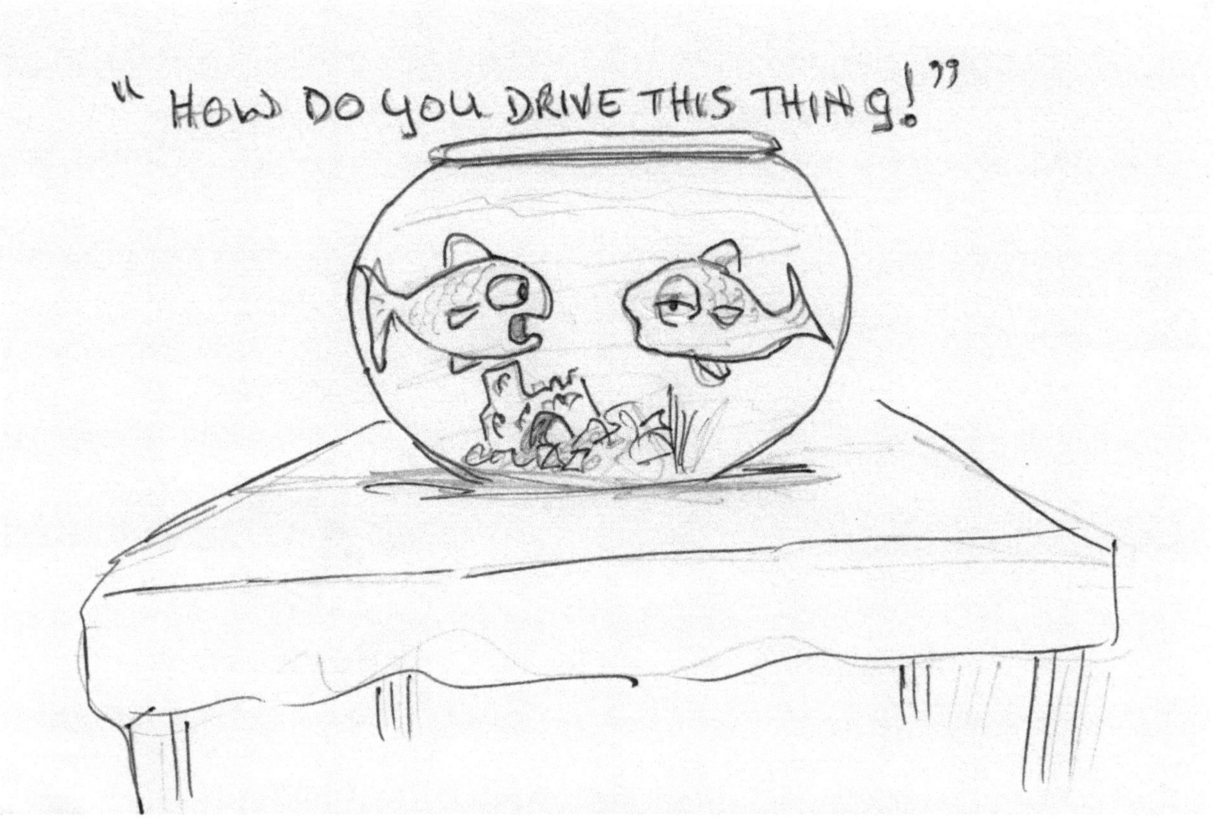
"HOW DO YOU DRIVE THIS THING!"

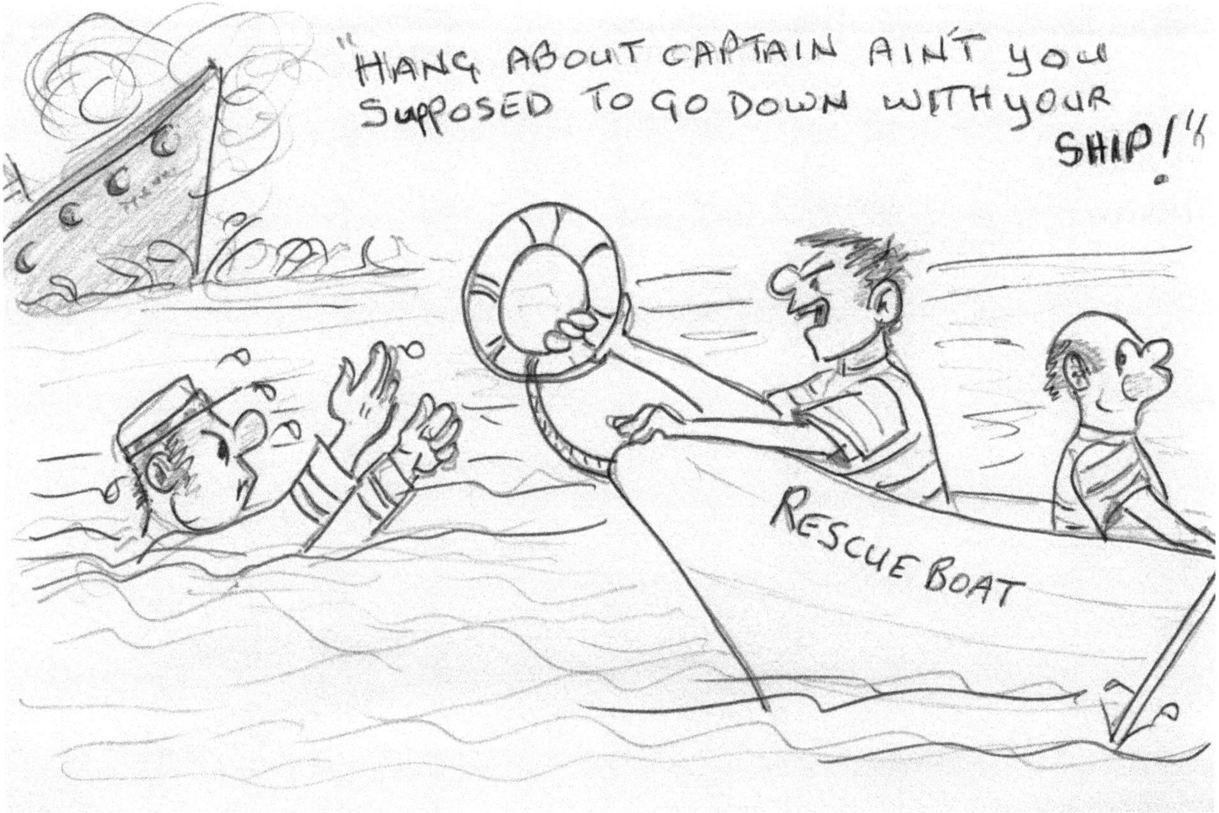
"HANG ABOUT CAPTAIN AIN'T YOU SUPPOSED TO GO DOWN WITH YOUR SHIP!"
RESCUE BOAT

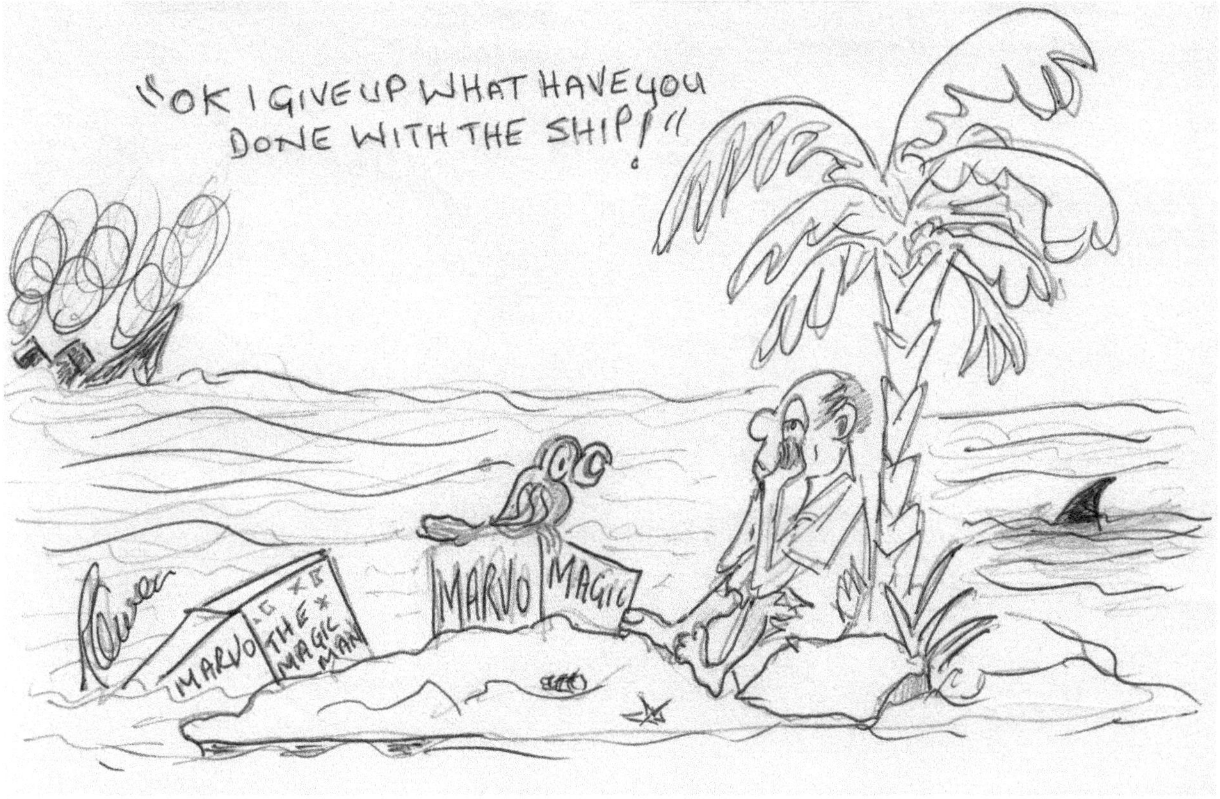
"OK I GIVE UP WHAT HAVE YOU DONE WITH THE SHIP!"
MARVO THE MAGIC MAN
MARVO MAGIC

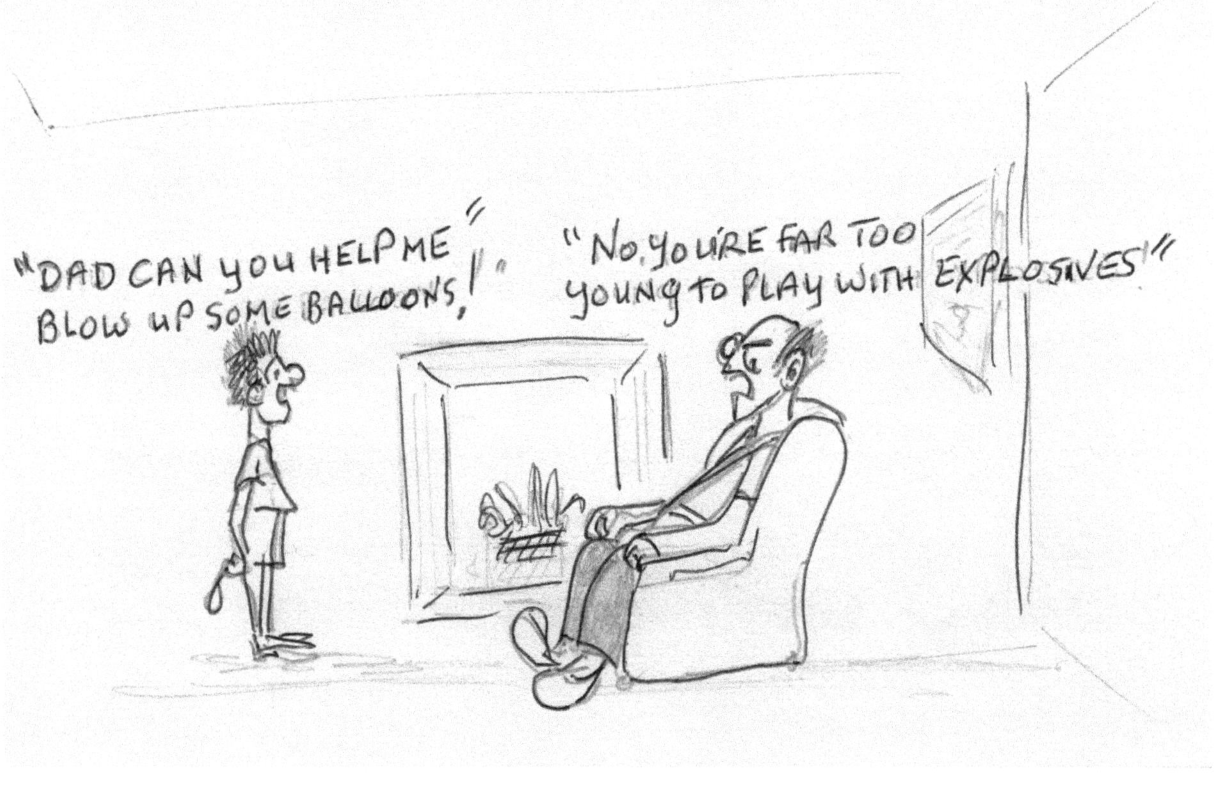
"DAD CAN YOU HELP ME BLOW UP SOME BALLOONS!"
"NO, YOU'RE FAR TOO YOUNG TO PLAY WITH EXPLOSIVES"

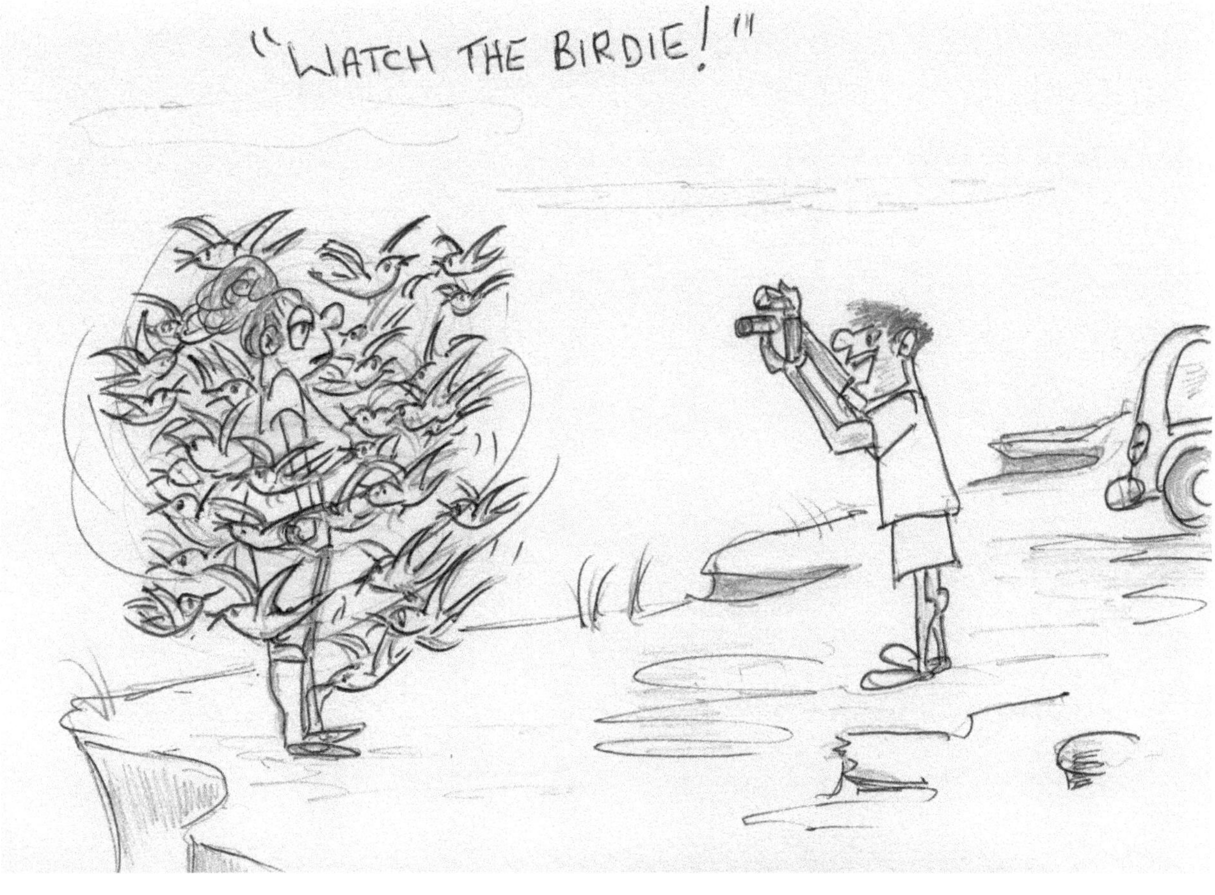
"WATCH THE BIRDIE!"

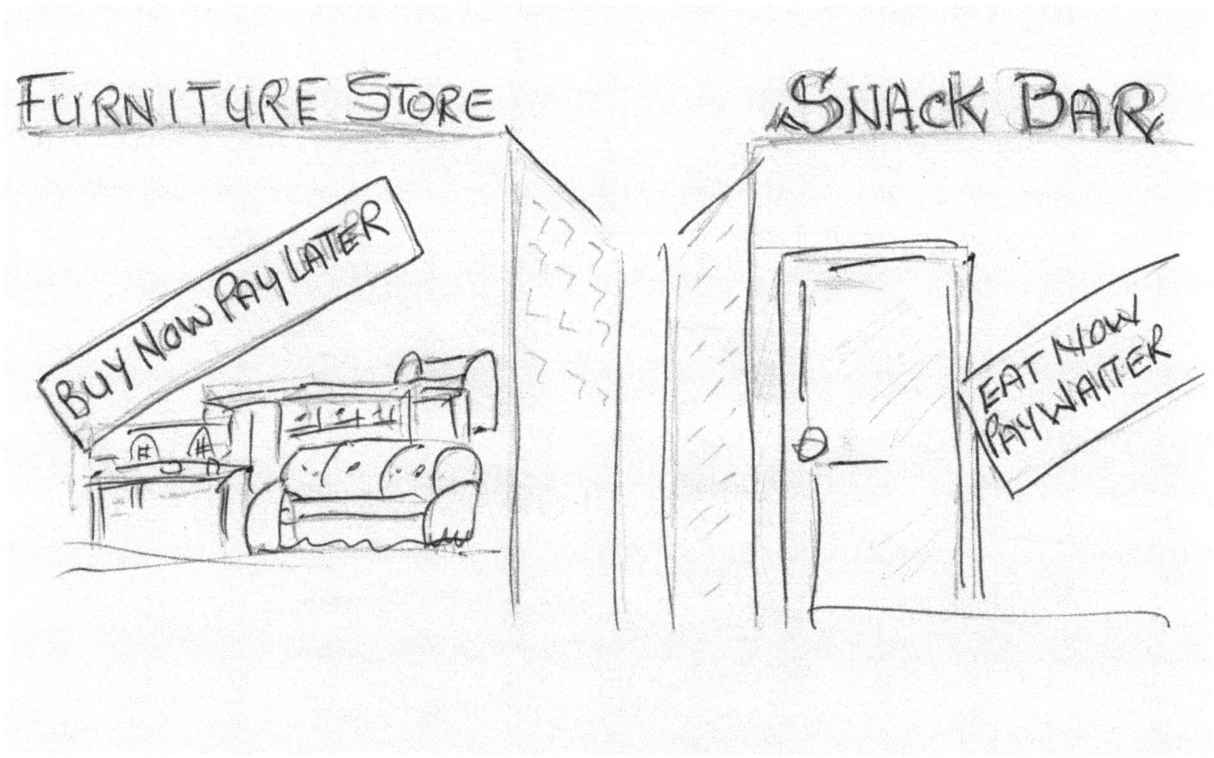
FURNITURE STORE
BUY NOW PAY LATER
SNACK BAR
EAT NOW PAY WAITER

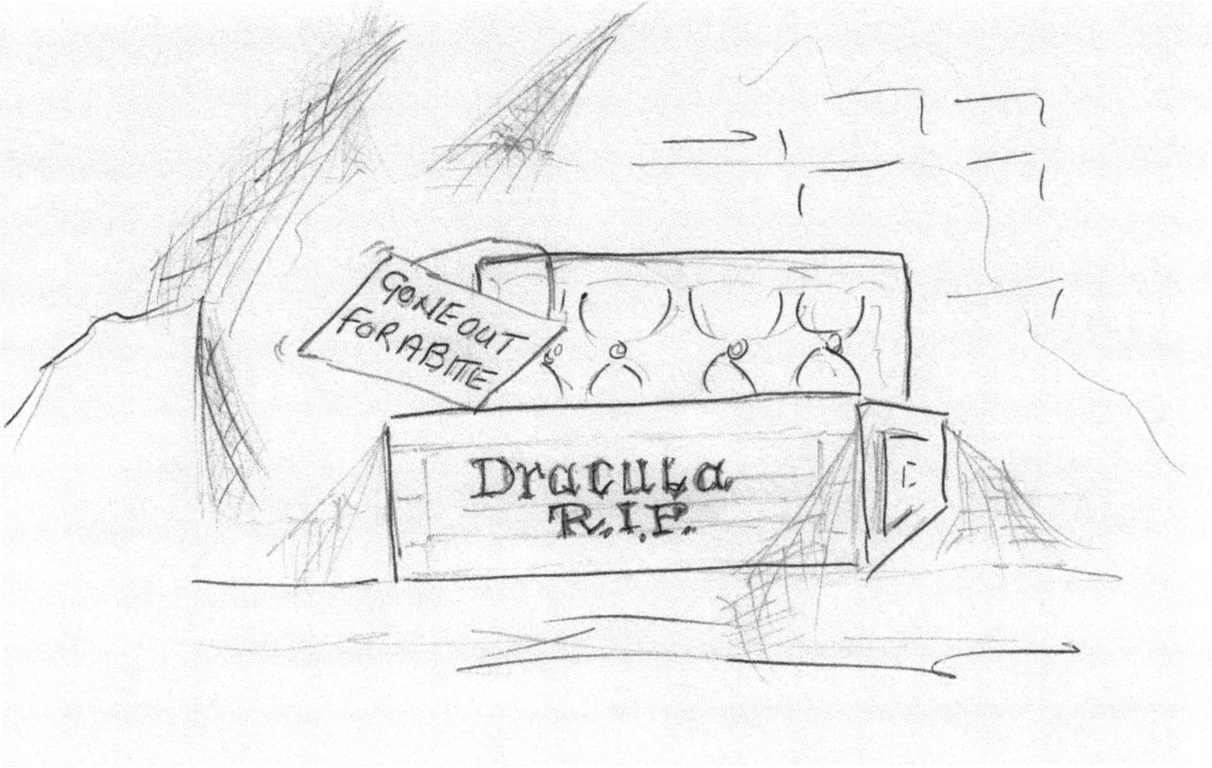
GONE OUT
FOR A BITE
Dracula
R.I.P.

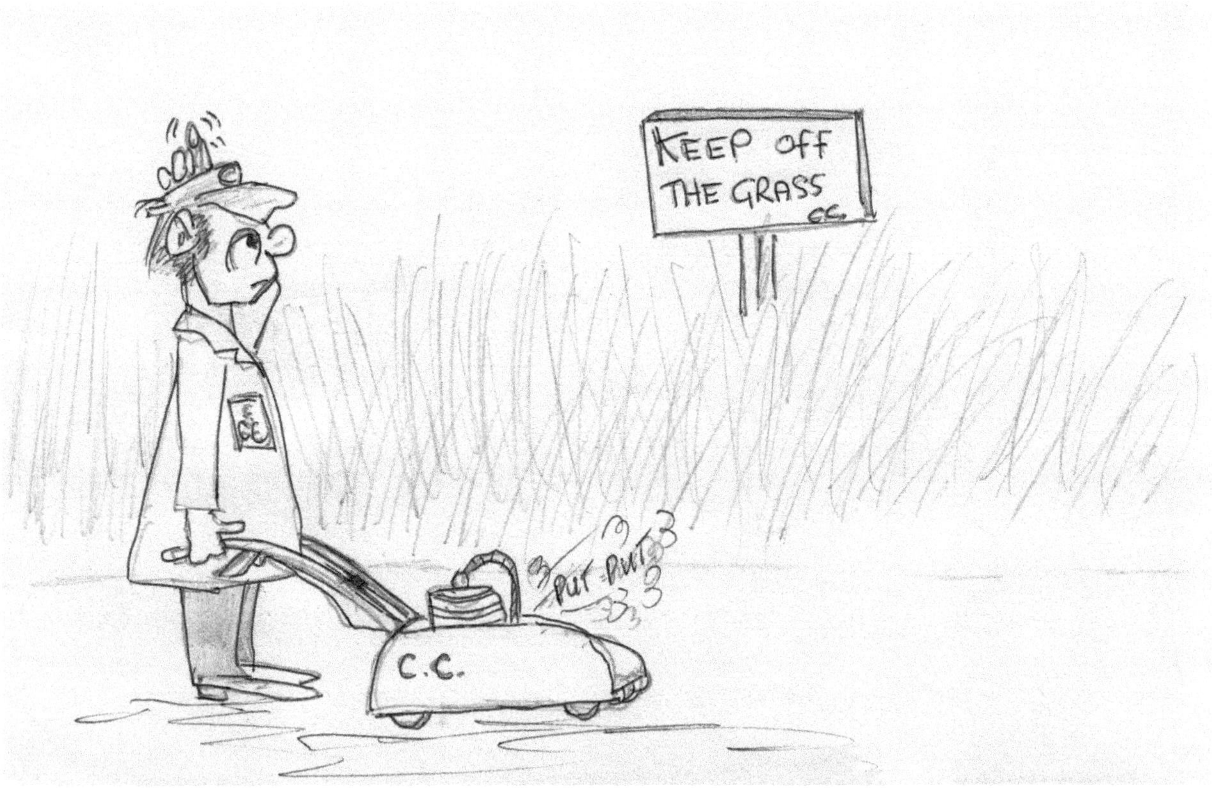
KEEP OFF
THE GRASS
C.C.
PUT PUT
C.C.

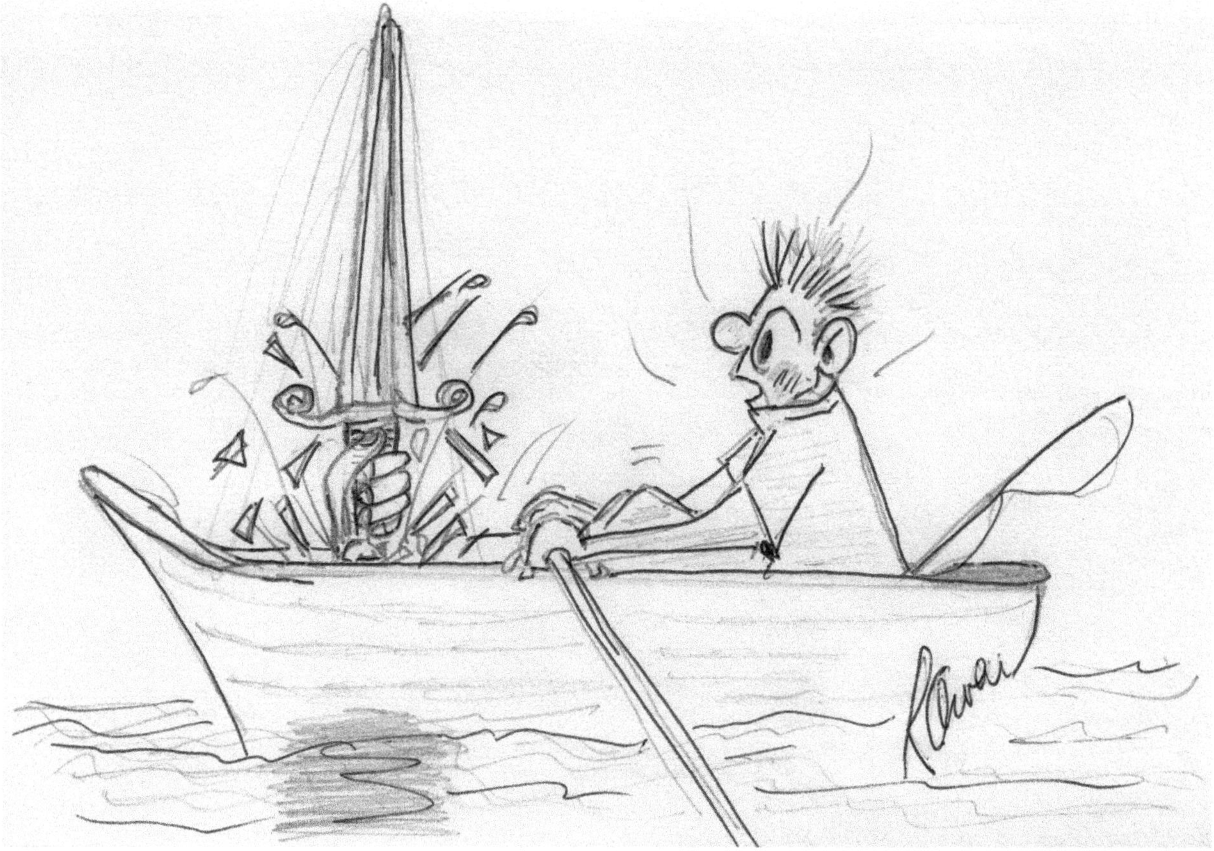
Rawai

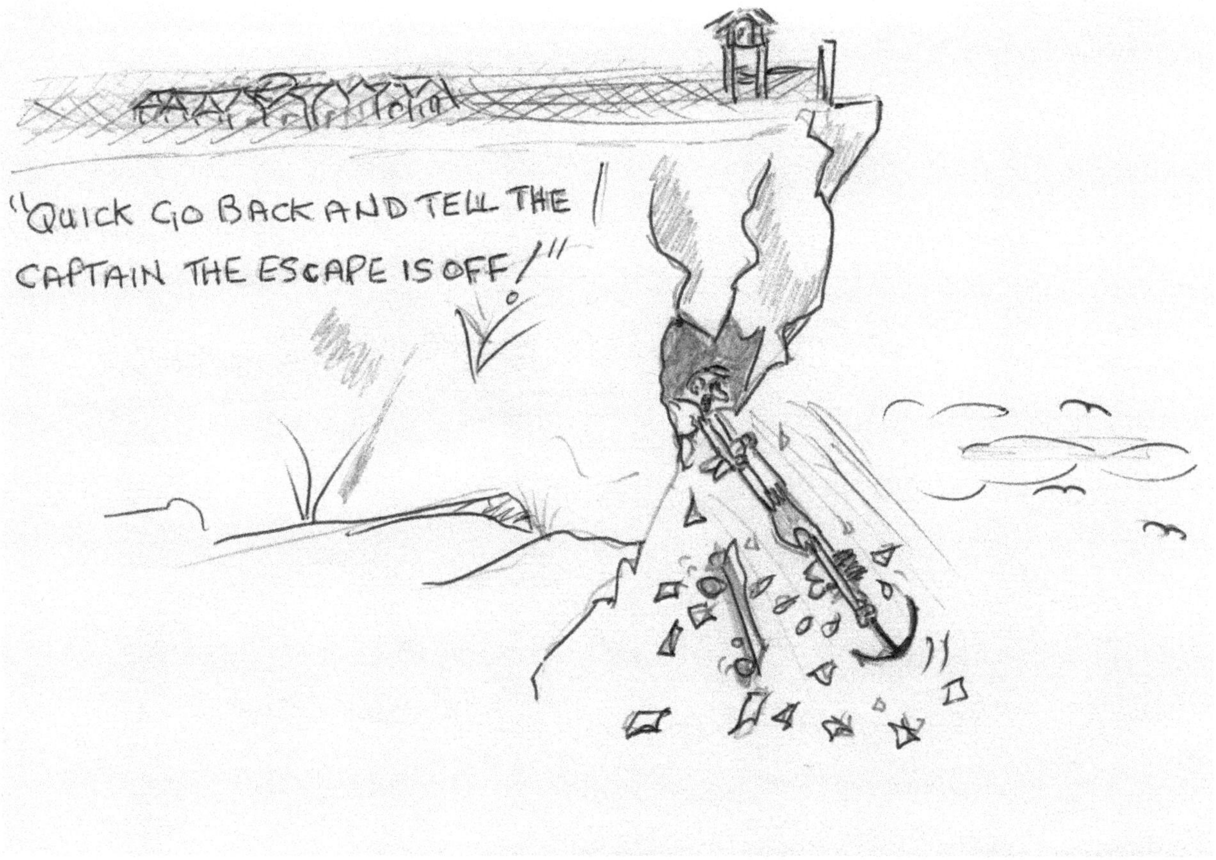
"QUICK GO BACK AND TELL THE CAPTAIN THE ESCAPE IS OFF!"

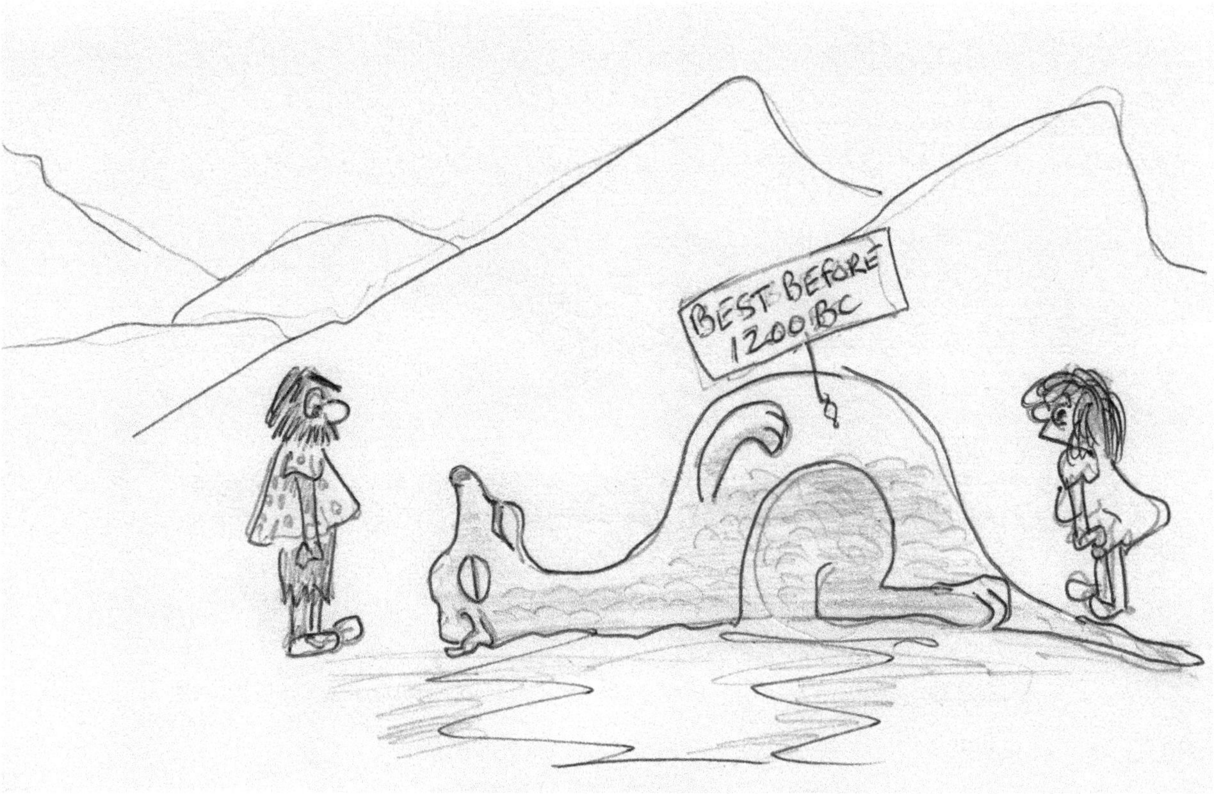
BEST BEFORE
1200 BC

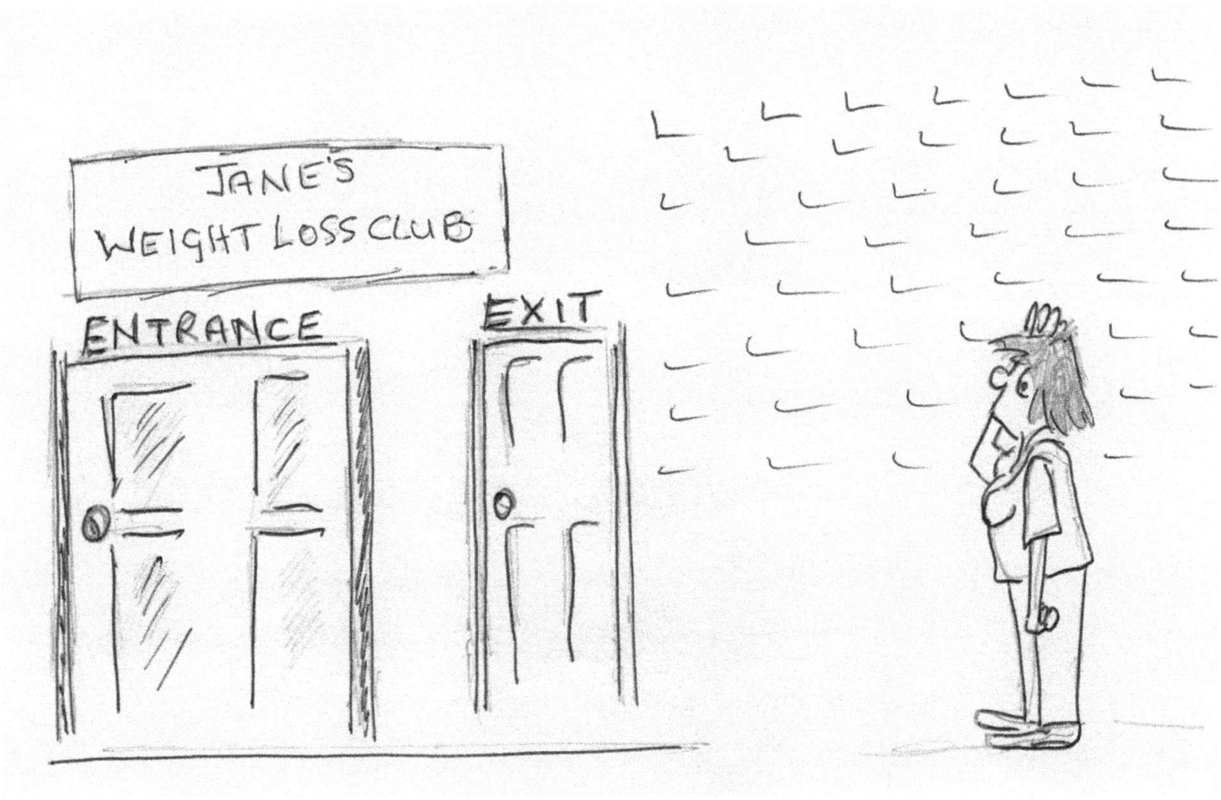
JANE'S
WEIGHT LOSS CLUB
ENTRANCE
EXIT

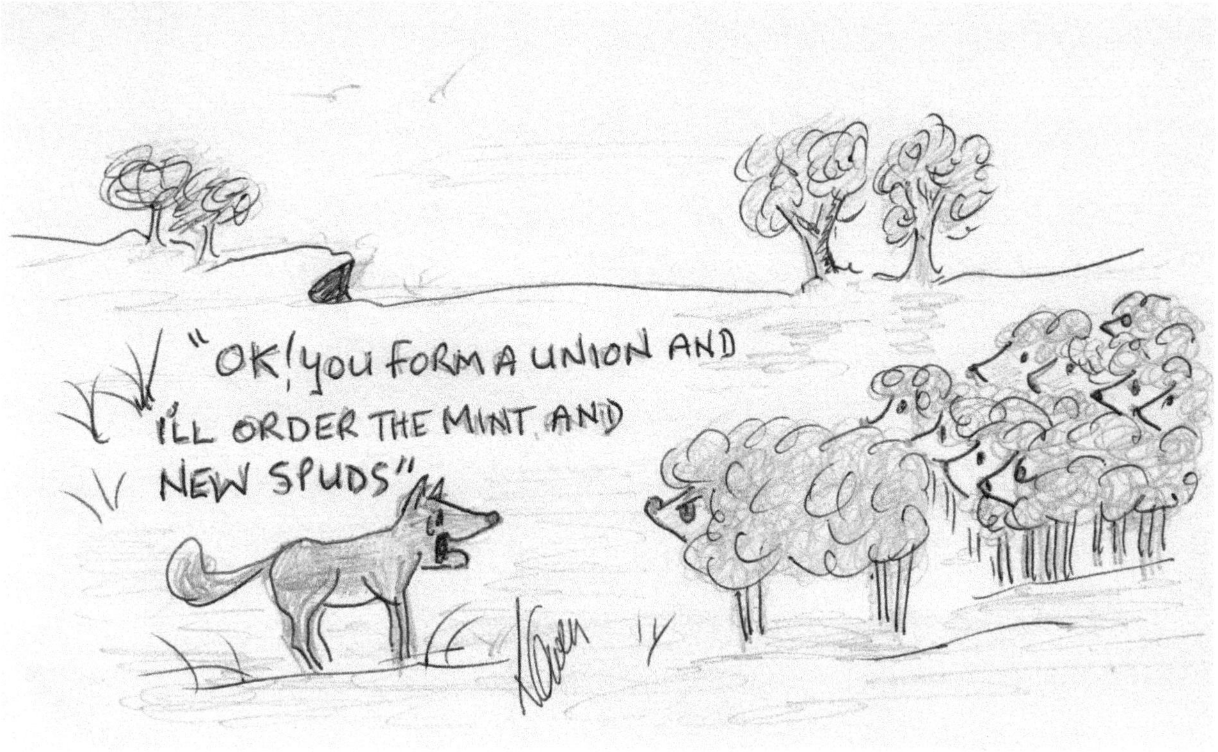
"OK! YOU FORM A UNION AND I'LL ORDER THE MINT AND NEW SPUDS"

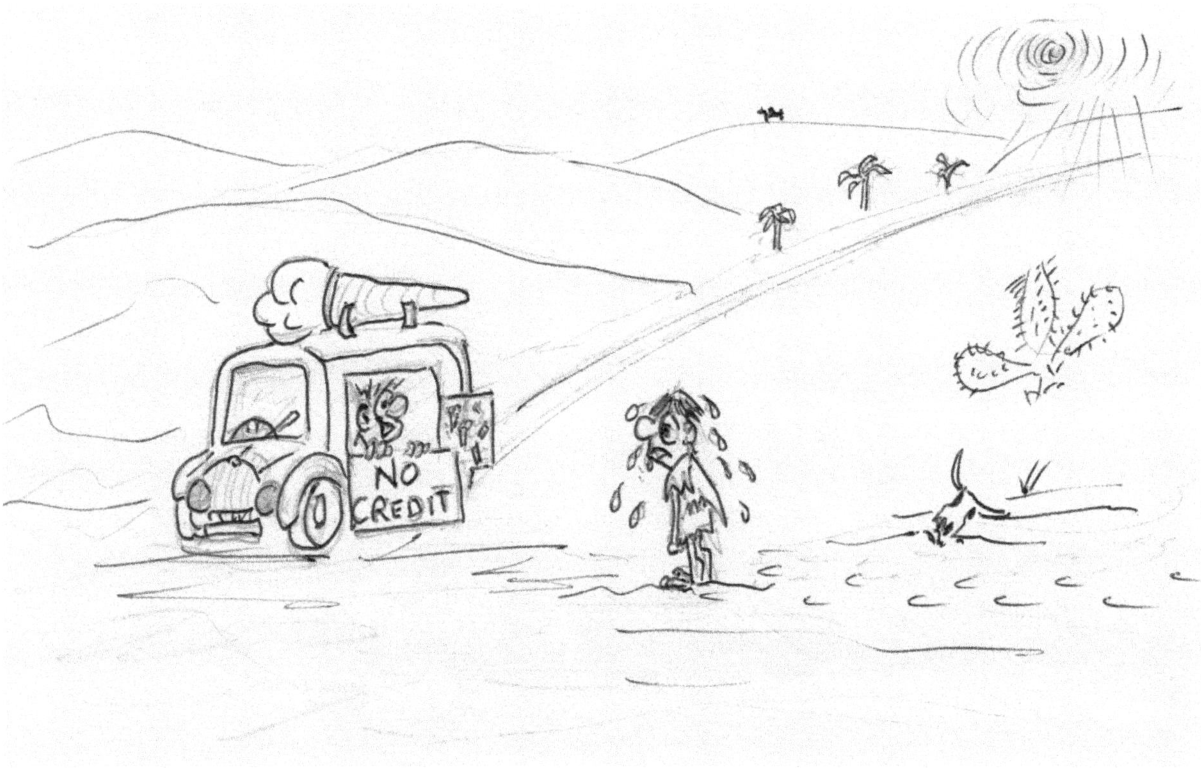
NO
CREDIT

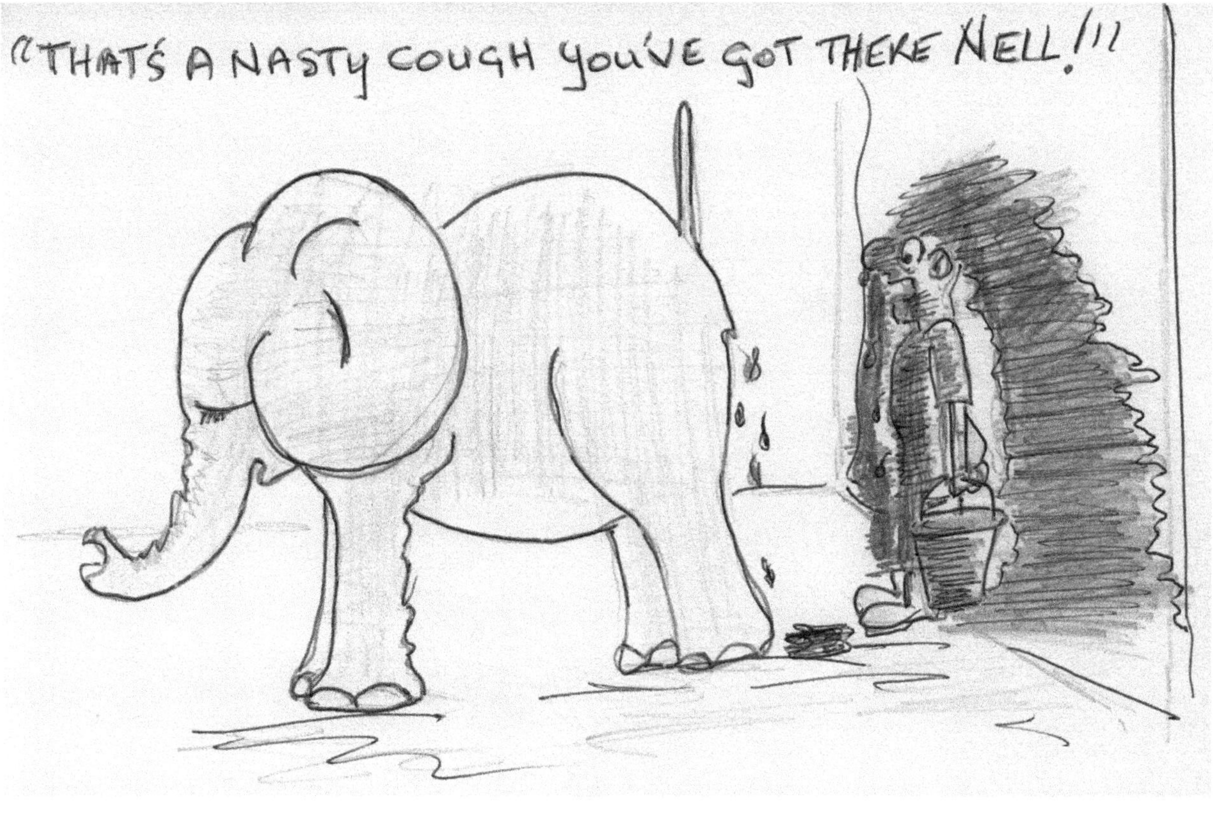
"THAT'S A NASTY COUGH YOU'VE GOT THERE NELL!"

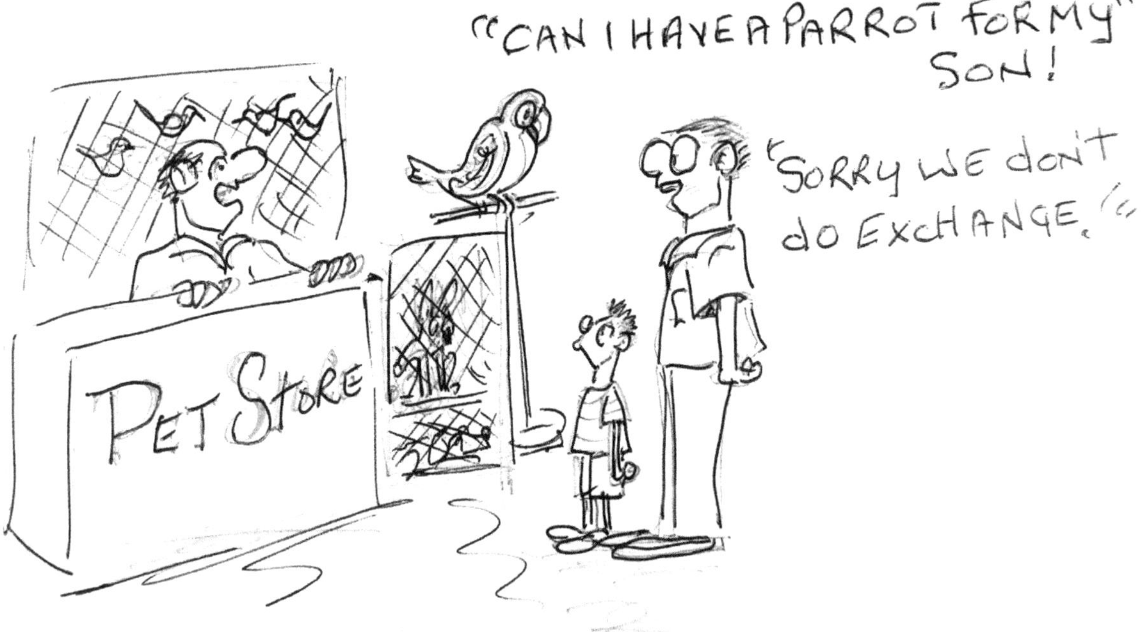
"CAN I HAVE A PARROT FOR MY" SON!
"SORRY WE don't do EXCHANGE."
PET STORE

"You'll HAVE TO STOP CALLING IN YOUR SLEEP TARZAN!"

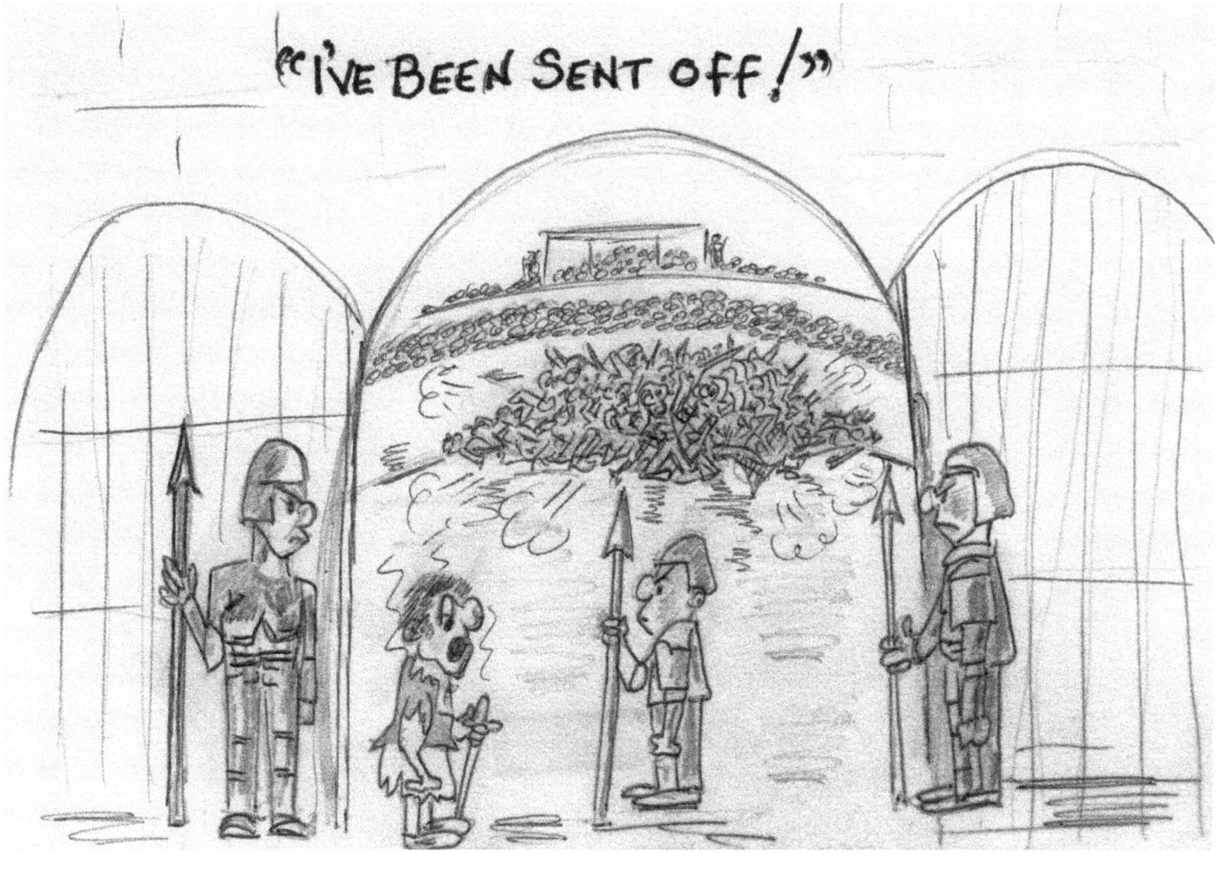
"I'VE BEEN SENT OFF!"

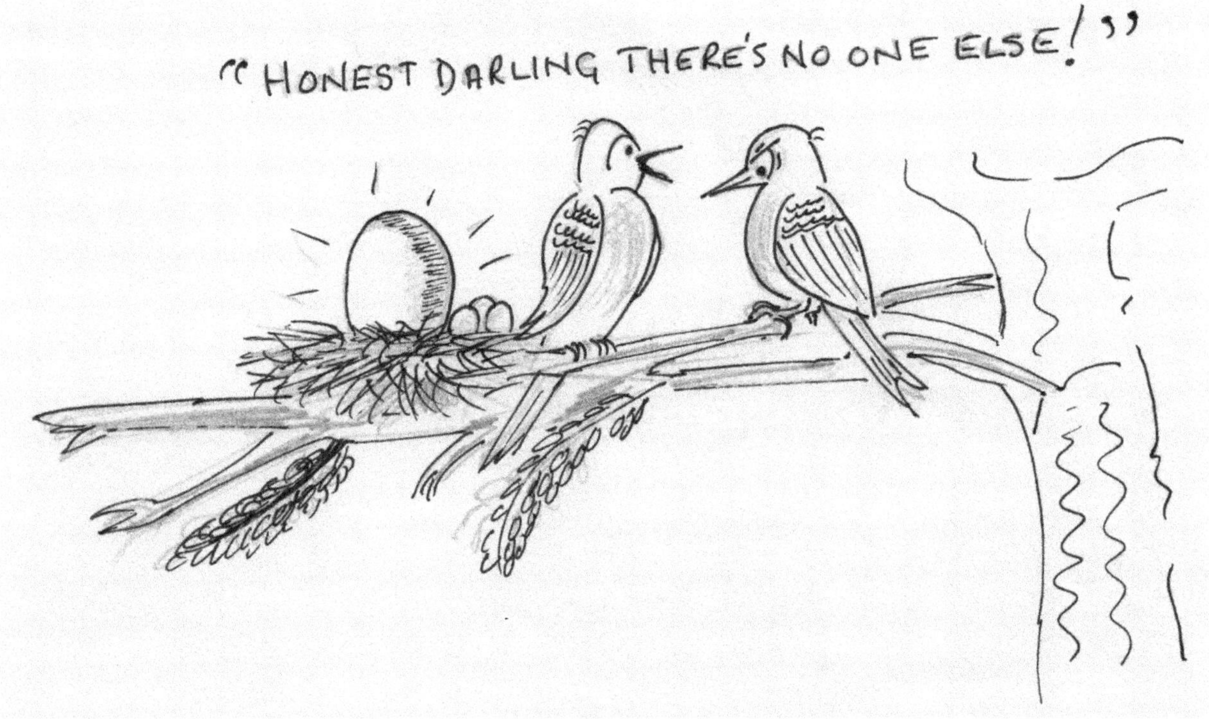
"HONEST DARLING THERE'S NO ONE ELSE!"

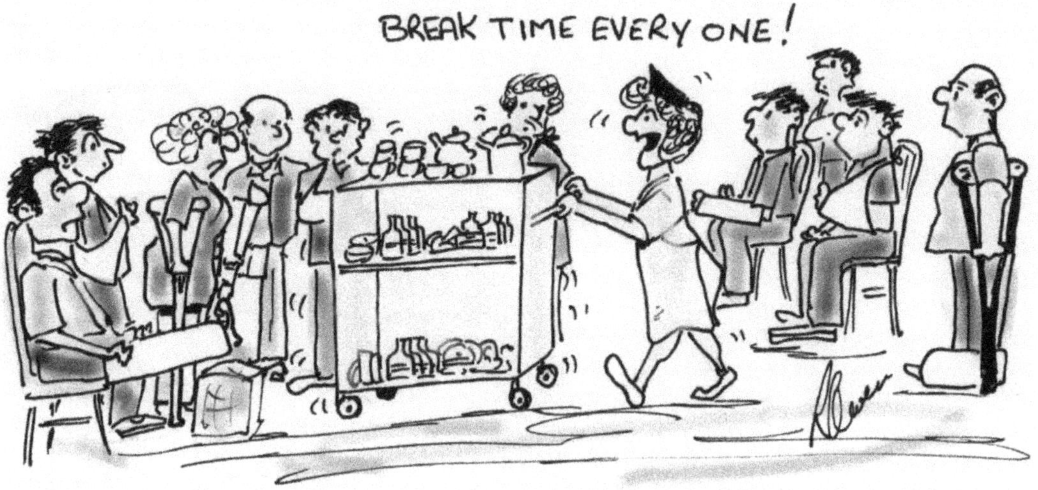
BREAK TIME EVERY ONE!

"NOW THAT'S WHAT I CALL A SALESMAN!"

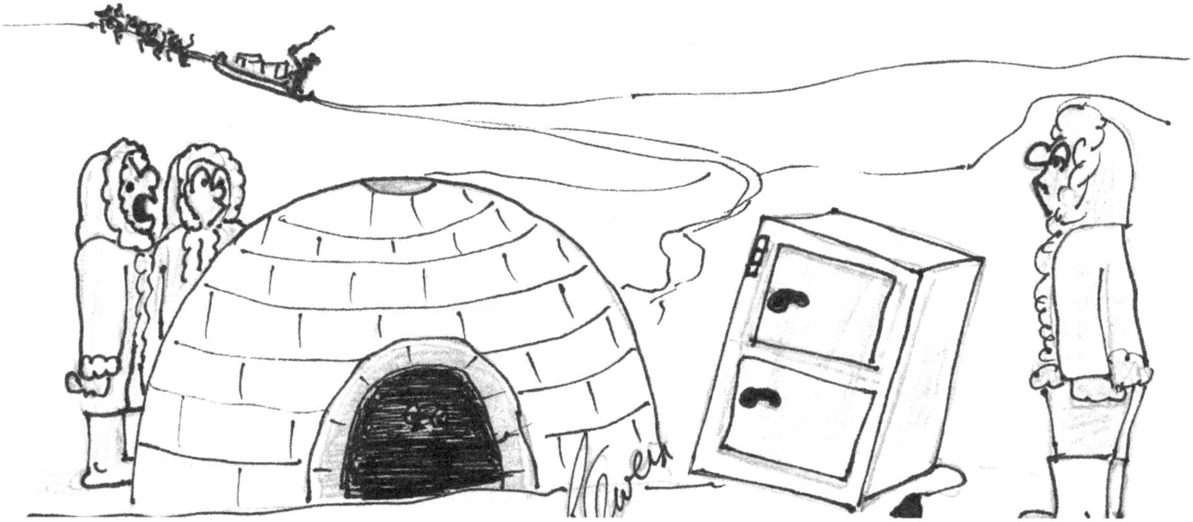

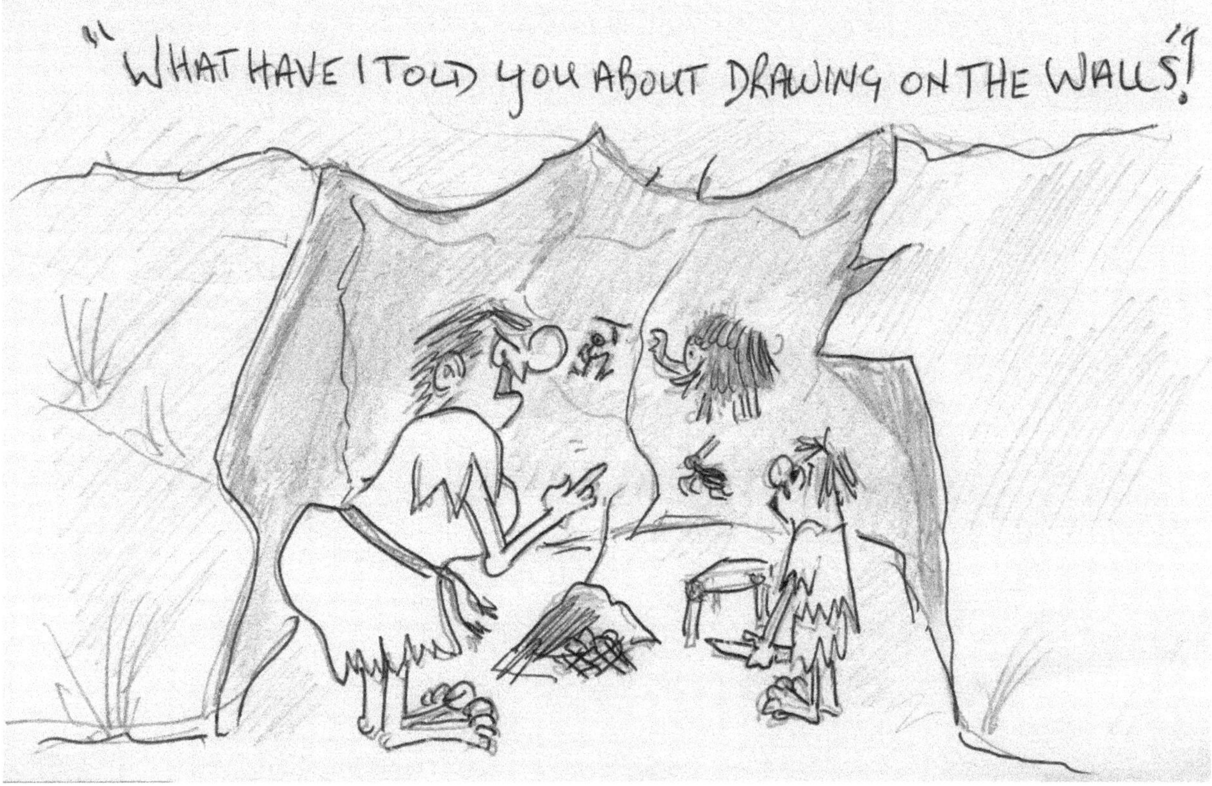
"WHAT HAVE I TOLD YOU ABOUT DRAWING ON THE WALLS!"

Lightning Source UK Ltd.
Milton Keynes UK
UKHW050729310522
403767UK00003B/15